Workbook
Basic News Writing

Workbook
Basic News Writing

Melvin Mencher
Columbia University

wcb
Wm. C. Brown Company Publishers
Dubuque, Iowa

Contents

Preface

The only way to learn to write is to write. This workbook will give you the chance to develop your writing skills by sharpening them on a variety of exercises. The exercises cover a wide range of activities, the same kinds of events that reporters handle in their daily work.

Many of these exercises are based on actual events. When you complete your story, your instructor will help you compare it with the work of the reporter who actually wrote the story. At first, there will be only the slightest resemblance. Don't lose heart. Journalists learn by doing, and as you progress through the course you will find that you are moving closer and closer to the professional level.

Prepare copy carefully. Instructions for copy preparation are given in the textbook. Double-check names, ages, addresses and other facts to make sure you are accurate. Do the best you can on every story, short and long, even on those that seem routine to you. The good news writer can make almost any story interesting.

Good luck.

Part 1

Journalists in Action

1 In the Newsroom and on the Beat

Exercises I: Developing the Story Idea

In the following exercises, find the important idea or ideas in the information supplied. If helpful, jot down the ideas using a single phrase for each. If you have selected one idea, make it the basis of the lead. If you have selected more than one, put the ideas in order of importance and write a lead based on the most important one or combine two for the lead. Then write the rest of the story. Make certain to check facts that you think may be questionable or may need explanation.

A. Memorial

The mayor's press secretary, Leon Roper, calls to tell you that a softball game will be played on the Horace Mann baseball field Sunday at 2 p.m. between a team composed of city officials and workers and members of the local chamber of commerce. No admission will be charged, but contributions will be solicited for the Chris Hatfield Memorial Fund. Hatfield was the city manager for three years and died last August of cancer at the age of 31. The fund goes toward cancer research. Cliff Guzman, the secretary of the chamber, will pitch for his team, and Albert Heffner, the city budget director, will throw curves for the officials.

B. Zoo

Information from Cyrus Tucek, the director of the zoo: The Newman Municipal Zoo has purchased two animals, a 6,000-pound female African elephant and a burro. After becoming accustomed to their surroundings, the animals will be put on exhibit. The elephant is named Baby and was obtained from the Brookfield Zoo in Chicago. The burro, which will be added to the Children's Zoo, is from the H. Gage Ranch in northern New Mexico and will be named by children who use the zoo. Suggested names will be put on a bulletin board and the children will vote. Names put up by zoo workers are: Pancho, Rodney, Eeyore, Captain B, Secretariat, Taco, Chico, Cyrus, Mr. Cronkite and Cyrano.

Tucek also said the zoo is considering the use of birth control methods to keep its tiger population down. The female tigers have been producing litters of three to five cubs every 10 months, he said, and the zoo has no room for them. Nor will other zoos accept the young tigers. "They're full up, too, and are using a time-release contraceptive implanted under the skin for females and vasectomies for males.

"Lions, tigers and leopards are disappearing in the wilds and proliferating in zoos and wildlife parks so fast there's no room for them," Tucek said.

C. Laundromat

Police report: Jerome Pardee, 20, 1874 Ogden St., arrested and charged with public drunkenness. Found naked in a laundromat at 402 Newell Ave. at 11 p.m. yesterday, Pardee told police that he planned to put his clothing back on as soon as the automatic washer was finished with them. Police had to wait 30 minutes for the cycle to finish before they could take him in.

D. Weather

The weather bureau said temperatures over the past 24 hours ranged from 25 at 5 a.m. to 40, the high, at 2 p.m. This was the third straight day of unseasonably cold weather. This morning's temperature of 25 was the lowest for this time of year in 15 years. The all-time low for the date was in 1880, 15 degrees. The all-time high was 69. The forecast for today is for lows in the 40's, highs in the 50's and an end to the sudden cold snap.

E. Fire

The fire department reports two small fires overnight: a storeroom blaze at the A&P at 135 Kentucky St., 10:30 p.m., cause unknown, damage $450 in canned goods; fire in car in garage at 630 Orcutt Ave., 11 p.m., cigarette ignited papers on car seat, $600 damage to car. Dennis Held, car owner who lives at Orcutt address, treated for minor burns at Community Hospital. Wife saw smoke and pulled him from car. He had fallen asleep listening to end of baseball game.

F. Ombudsman

Call from the governor's office: Bruce Stroh, a former high school basketball player in your city who was sentenced to 15 years in the state penitentiary for armed robbery 10 years ago, has been appointed state ombudsman for prisoners in state institutions. Governor made the announcement today from the state capitol. "Stroh will investigate prisoner complaints and report directly to the governor. This is a new system that is designed to make us more responsive to the needs of inmates," the governor said. Stroh was paroled five years ago and has worked as a probation officer. His father, Cedric Stroh, is a retired plumber and lives at 1215 Millbank Rd.

Exercises II: Finding the Theme

Under each slug are several facts about an event. Underline or circle the most important fact, the one you think best sums up the event and is of greatest reader or listener interest.

Then write a lead based on the underlined or circled material. Finally, write a news story.

A. Dispute

1. The Queens Mountain Rescue Squad and the Queens Mountain police chief have been in a controversy for a week.
2. Chief Lloyd Earl had ordered his men not to stop traffic at intersections to let ambulances through.
3. The squad, made up of volunteer rescue workers, felt the chief interfered with its work.
4. The rescue squad complained to Mayor Henry Joyner and to the Queens Mountain Board of Commissioners.
5. At an executive session of the mayor and the board last night, the chief resigned.

B. Taxes

1. Next year's proposed Gaston County budget calls for expenditures of $54.8 million.
2. This is $2.1 million more than the current budget.
3. Revenue collections will be about $1.4 million short of the expenditures next year.
4. David Hunscher, the county manager, supplied this information to the county board of commissioners last night in presenting his proposed budget.
5. Hunscher says that he made many cuts in budget requests from department heads and it will be difficult to make more.
6. The probability, he said, is that taxes will have to be raised.

C. Mail

1. T. J. Ellingson, an assistant United States postmaster general, issued a statement at a news conference today.
2. He said that the costs of running the postal service are constantly increasing.
3. "Further attempts must be made to cut costs," he said.
4. "One of the plans under consideration is twice-weekly home mail delivery and thrice-weekly deliveries to business."
5. Nothing is definite yet pending further examinations of the options, he said.

D. Shooting

1. Mrs. Bernice Joyce, 32, of 101 Rebecca Drive was arrested this morning at the home of her mother.
2. She was taken to criminal court and charged with shooting her husband, Coleman, last night during an argument.
3. The two had quarreled over her plans to divorce him.
4. He had returned to the house from a hotel where he was staying to try to persuade her to drop the divorce.
5. A fight ensued during which he was shot.
6. He is in critical condition at Fairlawn Hospital.
7. The charge is attempted homicide.

Exercises III: Copy Editing

Before handing in news stories reporters examine them to correct errors in grammar, punctuation, spelling and word usage and to make the style conform to the stylebook for abbreviations, capitalizations and the like. Names, addresses, titles and figures are double-checked for accuracy.

Stories are always read twice before they are turned in.

If changes are to be made in paragraph order, the part of the story to be shifted is retyped and pasted into the correct place, or the paragraph is cut out and pasted in. Lines or arrows are **not** used to indicate changes in order.

Corrections and additions are **printed,** not written in longhand. Chapter 10 in the textbook contains a guide to copy editing symbols.

Copy Marking

capitalize	U. S. district court judge Frank	District Court Judge
transpose / insert word	J. Broyles will hear arguments oral ∧ *Monday*	oral arguments / Monday
delete word and close up	on a suit ~~Monday~~ filed by a woman	suit filed
correction	who wants to build a new Mont∧ssori *e*	Montessori
new paragraph	School east of Freeport. ⌐Jane	
lower case / separate	Fraker Levine, President of a	president / of a

3

insert apostrophe / insert comma	childrens group filed suit last week	children's / group, filed
delete letter and close up	alledging that city officials illegally	alleging
separate / bring together	revokeda building permit she said s he	revoked a / she
spell out	obtained last July from the (CHA) for	City Housing Authority
abbreviate	the school at 301 Maple (Avenue)	Ave.
abbreviate	In January, the (City Housing Authority)	CHA
use figures	said it had (eleven) objectives but	11
retain/ addition	decided ~~to~~ issue _the permit_ anyway.	to / the permit

A. Kliff

A 22-year-old man was chared with reclessly driving last night after a high-speed chase from Pleasant

Valley road, past albright Avenue and up to the driveway of his home.

The man, Paul A. Kliff, 22, of 29 Tudor St., was to be arranged on district court today.

Police said a Police Cruiser gave chase when the suspect's auto was seen speeding on Valley Rd.

When it was stopped finally in the driveway at Tudor St., police said, Kliff removed himself of his auto

and began to struggle with officers as a crowd of people gathered.

B. Dumped

Michael Canzian, deputy A. G., charged today that the states' menatl institutions are being used as

"dumping grounds for senior citzens and alcoholocs."

Canzian estimaed that it costs the state approximately $15,000 a year for each mental patient now "incarcerated" in State institutions over the state. He said the attorney generl's affice has filed suit against sveral hospitals to call attention to the situation. He hopes that the suits will go to trial in the spring of next year.

"Too many people whose only problem is ther age have been sent to mental homes", he said in a talk to the Golden Years Club at its clubhouse at 56 Forester Road.

C. Spring

A menu of wet snow, slush and rain—gurnished with glum and fog—was dished up to Maryland residents today as the state struggled to switch from winter to Spring.

Whereas most of the state was doused with rain, northwestern areas received not-unsubstantial amounts of snow. The record for the sudden return to winter was May 9, of 1977, when the regeion recieved eleven inches, an event that caused power failures and alot of traffic problems throughout the state.

State police said there was no major traffic problems state-wise. Sanding crews took care of the slush and ice that piled up on highways police said.

D. Trees

The planing of trees on long-barren city streets will be slowed considerably this year because the amount of federal funds available for the work of planting is much less than last year, when almost 3,000 street trees were planted throughout the city.

City Forester John T. Voboril said he hopes to plant about 1,000 trees this year, but he said he is

not sure that enough money will be available to reach that goal of 1000 tree plantings.

Because of this uncertainty, Voboril said he has temporarily halted work on a survey to ascertain

which streets are most in need of new trees.

Last year the city used a $400 thousand dollar public works grant from the Federal Government to

pay for about 2,000 trees, and planted about 1,000 more with funds provided by the Mayor's Office of

Community Development (MOCD).

But the Federal Government is not offering public works grants this year. So the city has to rely

solely on its community development fund for tree plantings.

Voboril said he requested $200,000 from the county development office for street trees, enough for

about 1,000 plantings. But has not been told yet whether he will get this amount.

2 Focus on the Journalist

Exercises I

A. Golfers

You are on the sports desk of the local newspaper when a call comes in from a stringer assigned to Freeport to cover the state Women's Amateur Golf Meet in which several local women are entered.
 She dictates the following:

Here's a rundown of local players' first round play for the tourney. I also got their addresses and ages:

Mrs. Leonard Levy, 39, 54 Maplewood Ave., shot an 83.
Mrs. William Downey, 42, 165 Vincent St., 87.
Mrs. B. Kroeger, 32, 880 Augusta Ave., 77.
Mary Ellen Flynn, 18, Roth Road, 77.
Sally Grubbs, 17, Smith Farms, 71.

Sally shot a hole-in-one on the seventh hole, and I went over to interview her after her first round. It was the only hole-in-one today, and they say it is the first one on this course by a woman in five years since a visiting pro did it on the same seventh hole.

Sally is a senior at Eisenhower High School and is going to go to the University of Missouri. Her mother and father were here and they were pleased as punch. Her dad, Oscar Grubbs, said he gave her a putter when she was three and "she never stopped swinging it." She sank it with a four iron on the 145-yard par-three hole.

Says Sally: "The ball hit on the front of the green just to the right and the ball rolled smoothly into the cup. It looked good when I hit it, right on the line, but I never thought it would go in.

"It's my first since I was seven and played on a kiddie course. My nine-year-old sister, Kay, was here today and she brings me good luck."

Sally didn't compete at all last year. This is her first big tourney. The leaders: Terry Pauli, 70; Carol Trucco, 71; Sally Grubbs, 71; Carolyn Oshiro, 72; Janet Bakinski, 73; Maureen Gerson, 75; Tamara Cort, 75; Joan Bodnar, 75; Diane Stark, 76; Tess Walters, 76.

The concluding round will be played tomorrow.

B. Changes

School superintendent Herbert Gilkeyson announces the following personnel changes that will affect the teaching staff next year:

Adele Bartles moves from sixth-grade English to vocational adviser, South Side High School. Mrs. Bartles took courses over the past three years at the state university and earned her M.A. in counseling.

Daniel Fox, physical education instructor in the Horace Mann School, appointed assistant principal of the school. His teaching post has been filled by Albert Pardone, of Flagstaff, Ariz., who graduated from the university there after three years as a member of the basketball and football teams.

Ron Phealan, fourth-grade teacher in George Packer Elementary School, has resigned to become a driver for Continental Trailways. He had taught in the system since 1974 and submitted his resignation two months ago citing his need for higher pay.

Michael Lang, Peoria, Ill., hired to replace Phealan after three years at the American School in Warsaw, Poland, where he taught elementary school. He is a graduate of the University of Georgia and is 31. Married, two children, 7 and 3.

C. Belmont

The city editor tosses the following three releases on your desk and asks you to rewrite them for today's paper.

Belmont Hotel
1579 Avenue of the Dolphins
765–4321
P. Lyon, Director of Press Relations

FOR IMMEDIATE RELEASE

The Belmont Hotel today announced an underwater extravaganza will be held next month in Freeport in the hotel's magnificent Turquoise Pool, which is the world's largest indoor swimming area.

The festivities will include entertainment by a bevy of colorful motion picture and television stars and starlets. Beginning June 21st and running through the 23rd, the activities will include a water show to begin the gala weekend on Friday at 8 p.m. Paul Nissen's Bathing Beauties, 12 pretty and curvaceous swimming stars, will open the weekend with coordinated swimming and diving. Their home base is Miami, Fla.

Saturday will feature former Olympic swimming greats Frieda Schwartz of Berlin and Mark Switzer of Switzerland, who will combine their talents to offer a magnificent display of underwater acrobatics. Following their show at 1 p.m., competitions will be held for all hotel guests in various swimming categories: 100-yard dash (under 21 years of age; 21–35; and senior citizens); backstroke (same categories); diving from high and low platforms (open). Winners will receive all-expense weekends in the Belmont Hotel.

Sunday, there will be personal appearances by Buster C. Rabbe and Holly (Kitten) Grove, a toddler's wading contest in the children's pool and other activities.

Albert Gill Associates
Public Relations Consultants
Times-Mirror Plaza
Los Angeles, Calif.

The underwater film festival scheduled for next month in Freeport will add another well-known aqua-star to its imposing list of cinematic and television greats. Buster C. Rabbe, star of the TV drama, "Seafarer," will appear next month to demonstrate a new lightweight underwater movie camera made by the Hashki Industries of Toyko, creators of the famous Hashki-O, the official underwater camera which will be used to film the festival.

(Radio announcers note: Rabbe is pronounced Rab, as in dab.)

Triple A Ads, Inc.
From: Barney Bishop
To: Freeport News, exclusive.

A vivacious Georgia Peach will be one of the stars at the underwater extravaganza scheduled for next month in the Belmont Hotel's Turquoise Pool, the world's largest indoor swimming pool.

Holly (Kitten) Grove will attend the film festival, straight from the West Coast.

Now pursuing her career in Hollywood, Kitten has crowded a number of exciting activities into her 19 years.

Born into a Southern family that traces its lineage back to the Scotch Highlanders, Kitten began winning beauty contests at the age of 16. Among her laurels are runner-up, Athens Press Photography Beauty Queen; Athens High School Miss Cut-Up; Freshman Beauty Queen, University of Georgia; Miss Revlon; Maid of Cotton semi-finalist; Miss Salvo, Naval ROTC, University of Georgia; and many others.

Kitten, a bountiful 36–24–36, has appeared on several television shows.

Exercises II: Finding the Theme

Underline or circle the most important fact or facts. Then write a lead and a news story.

A. Drive

1. Sara F. Glasser, president of the local chapter of the American Civil Liberties Union, announces a new membership drive.
2. The chapter usually solicits members by mail and telephone.
3. Next month, the drive will be made on a person-to-person basis to gain 50 new members.
4. Members and volunteers will be asked to invite friends to their homes to acquaint them with the ACLU.
5. "The chapter hopes to increase its membership to replace those who have dropped out and moved away," she said.
6. "If we cannot do so, we must discontinue the chapter," she said.

B. Gas

1. The supply of natural gas to Wisconsin has been going down for the past five years.
2. The state Public Service Commission has warned natural gas customers that the situation will steadily worsen.
3. Today, the Wisconsin Gas Co. announced it is halting all further commercial and industrial gas hookups.
4. It also announced it is submitting a plan to the PSC to reduce gas deliveries to some present customers during temporary shortages.
5. The utility will continue to serve its 356,000 customers in central and eastern Wisconsin.
6. The cutbacks were necessary, the firm says, because of continued natural gas shortages and an anticipated further reduction in available supplies next year.

C. Tennis

1. The annual Freeport Tennis Clinic will be held Aug. 21–24.
2. The clinic will feature exhibitions and instruction.
3. This is the twelfth annual clinic, sponsored by six Freeport civic clubs.
4. Billie Jean King, holder of a number of tennis titles, will give a demonstration Aug. 23 at 2 p.m.
5. King will play local tennis pro Marty Friedman in a singles match and then will team up with Friedman to play a mixed doubled against Mr. and Mrs. James Wigglesworth, the state mixed-doubles champions.
6. Friedman made the announcement today.

D. Bicycle Trip

1. Two students are going by bicycle from Boston to Seattle this summer.
2. The University of Rochester announced the project in a news release.
3. Edward A. Nelson and Kenneth Hardigan, third-year students in the university medical school, will make the trip.
4. The project is designed to test the body's ability to adapt to intensive training, the university release states.
5. "Information gained from the cross-country ride is expected to provide data of value to physiology in general and to sports medicine in particular," the release states.
6. Nelson, of Kent, Conn., will be the test subject and Hardigan will accompany him.
7. Nelson will be tested before and after the trip, and along the way he will conduct frequent self-tests.

E. Guns

1. Albert Waring, of the Washington office of the National Coalition to Ban Handguns, spoke last night at a meeting sponsored by the League of Women Voters and the Business and Professional Women's Club in the Civic Auditorium.
2. About 150 persons attended.
3. He said, "415,000 Saturday Night Specials (cheap handguns) were sold last year."
4. "There are at least 40 million handguns now in private ownership in the United States, more guns than the armies of Europe possess," he told the audience.
5. He also said: "The consequence is a murder rate 200 times greater than in Canada, Great Britain, Israel, Japan and West Germany, countries where it is almost impossible for a private individual to secure a handgun.
6. "About 33,000 Americans died by the gun last year, half of them murder victims, 14,000 suicides, and 3,000 in accidents."
7. "About four-fifths of all gun murders in the United States are committed with handguns."
8. "A concerted effort will be made to defeat the local congressman, William Trenzier, who has stated he does not approve of banning handguns through federal legislation."

F. Brush-off

1. During the past two weeks several fights have taken place during baseball games in both leagues.
2. In most cases, the cause was the brush-back pitch, a ball that is intentionally pitched close to a batter.
3. The pitch is used to prevent hitters from taking a firm footing in the batter's box and to retaliate for similar pitches by the opposing pitcher
4. Two days ago managers were warned to cool off their players.
5. Sparky Anders, manager of the local team, does not like the warnings. He said today, "I think they've taken it to the point where they've made it too safe for everybody. I think you have to live a little dangerously. Without that, you take away some of the competitiveness."

3 Making of the News Story

Exercises

A. Craftsman

You are working on the news desk of the newspaper in Flagstaff, Ariz., and you receive this press release in the mail. Rewrite in under 100 words for your newspaper.

Detroit—Teenagers from Medford, Ore., and Arlington, Va., were the top winners today in the $38,000 Fisher Craftsman's Guild Scholarship Awards for Model Car Designs.

Eighteen awards were made.

Tom H. Semple, 19, Medford, Ore., won a $5,000 university scholarship for taking first place in the 16–20 age group with his original one-twelfth scale model of a black sports coupe.

Winner of a similar scholarship in the competition for boys between 11 and 15 years old was Richard R. John, 15, Arlington, Va. His entry was a blue and aqua hardtop sports car.

The awards will be made at a special luncheon for the winners, Nov. 15.

Each year hundreds of youths enter the competition for awards totaling $117,000, including the scholarships. The contest is sponsored by Fisher Body Division of General Motors. Runner-up in the senior division was Michael B. Antonick, Mount Vernon, Ohio, while John M. D'Mura, 13, Flagstaff, Ariz., took second place honors in the junior competition. Each received a $4,000 scholarship.

The other awardees:

Third Place—($3,000 scholarship)—Richard L. Beck, 20, Louisville, Ky., senior division; Melvin G. Gable, 14, Ypsilanti, Mich., junior division.

Fourth place—($2,000 scholarships)—Michael S. Reese, 16, Houston, Tex., senior division; Harry F. Mahe, Jr., 15, Brooklyn, N.Y., junior division.

B. Poet

You are covering the Bergen County Courthouse and a court employee tells you that the county court judge, Harvey Smith, has handed down a decision in rhyme and that it might make a good story. You check and find he has indeed written a poem consisting of 15 stanzas.

The decision was made in an appeal of a municipal court decision in Ridgefield Park in which Eugene T. Bohelska was fined $300 on his conviction for using profanity on the telephone, a violation of state law. Bohelska was also convicted of driving an improperly registered vehicle, although he contended he was driving someone else's car and should not have been held responsible. He appealed his conviction on the profanity charge, which grew out of an incident with the court clerk.

The incident began when, after two delays in his municipal court hearing on the driving charge, Bohelska called the court to ask for another delay. He said he was ill with a fever. The clerk refused to make a postponement and he allegedly cursed her. The clerk, Geraldine Mucella, then filed charges.

Here are the key stanzas from the judge's long poem:

DECISION:
Vulgar words transmitted by phone
Are not enough when standing alone
To land said caller in a jail cell
Where, for six months, he's
    required to dwell;
For while such words may cause some
    resentment
Their use is protected by the First
    Amendment.
Tempers then flared 'til it sounded the same
As a Rangers-Flyers hockey game.
"F——— you, go f——— yourself"
    Eugene blurted
Though use of that word should be averted.
Before the sentence was even completed
He wished that the expletive had been deleted.
You say things couldn't possibly worsen?
Well the clerk of the court was a female
    person.
Next day the cop in the hat rang the bell and
    waited
Eugene opened the door, his fever had abated.
He knew that he now would be printed and
    booked
Figured his goose was practically cooked.

They went to the station and straight to the
    jail
He stayed there til mother posted his bail
Title Two A, Chapter One Seventy, Section
    Twenty-nine (three)
Is the charge for which posting of bail set him
    free.
It provides that when using the telephone
Mere profanity standing alone
Even if stated in friendship or jest
Is a criminal act, hence the arrest.
The Ridgefield Park docket was busy that
    night
Traffic, this case and a big bar room fight.
Judge George A. Browne, if I may opine
Talks a lot like the late Gertrude Stein.
Justice was dispensed at a good rapid pace
Next thing you know they called Eugene's
    case.
There were few facts disputed, no witnesses
    lied
The question was "How would the law be
    applied?"
Judge George A. Browne made his position
    quite clear

He said that his clerk was shell pink of ear.
The words Eugene used were obscene and
　profane
And it caused her anguish and much mental
　pain.
For that telephone call with the curses and
　hollers
The fine imposed was three hundred dollars.
The lawyer protested and fought on with zeal
So now we turn to Eugene's appeal.
Can you swear if you hit your thumb with a
　hammer
Without risk of spending six months in the
　slammer?
When the bank computer errs and bounces
　your check
Is your language confined to aw gees and oh
　hecks?
Does the law require you to stand mute
While a cigarette burns a hole in your suit?
Is it reasonable to remain calm and composed
If the photograph shows your horse has been
　nosed?

Statutory attempts to regulate pure bluster
Can't pass what is called constitutional
　muster.
Use of vulgar words that may cause
　resentment
Is protected by the First Amendment.
There must be a danger of breach of the peace
For this near sacred right ever to cease.
This was no obscene call from a sick deranged
　stranger
Of a breach of the peace there was no possible
　danger.
Eugene hurled an expletive in sheer
　exasperation
And that isn't a crime anywhere in this nation.
The cop in the hat and Judge George A.
　Browne
Will read this opinion and grumble and frown.
They may ring me up just to holler and curse
But I still can't affirm. I have to reverse.

C. Answer

When the prosecutor, Joseph C. Woodcock Jr., whose office represented the state in the appeal, heard about the decision, he responded with a memo that you happen to pick up the next day. (See Exercise B. Poet.) Here is the memo:

> Judge Smith, you have rendered your opinion
> And you think that is that,
> But as for the prosecutor's office,
> We salute you and say
> ———— in your hat.

D. Violence

You are covering the annual conference of the American Advertising Federation for a press association and you hear that the vice president of one of the leading advertising agencies in the country, the J. Walter Thompson Company, will be speaking about violence on television.

The advertising executive, John Donaldson, reported at a seminar the results of a study by his agency. You obtain some of the findings:

> Ten percent of a sample of adult viewers considered not buying a product because it had been advertised on an excessively violent program.
> Eight percent said they actually had not purchased a product advertised because of the violence.

You obtain comments from those attending the conference. Most agree with the advertising executive for a Midwestern group of stations, Stellar Television, Inc., of Chicago, who identifies himself as Frank Denton. He tells you:

This is an extremely significant finding. If agencies believe this, then it's goodbye to those programs of blood and guts and gore. All the handwringing of the academicians and mothers' groups don't mean anything to the advertiser. Sales do. And a 10 to 20 percent cut in sales spells disaster. We are taking this very seriously. It will have an enormous impact on what millions of people see on their sets.

E. Center

The Zoning and Planning Board last night completed a hearing on the proposal of the Salvation Army for a community center at 740 Elm St. A decision is expected at the next meeting, Jan. 20.

At the hearing:

The army proposes to build a two-story center at a cost of $500,000. The army was promised the new location as part of a land swap in an urban renewal project whose planning was completed two years ago.

The present center is three blocks away. That land is part of a proposed mall.

Four merchants at 740 Elm oppose the board's granting approval. The owners are: Frank Chaffee, Frank's Deli; Margaret Williams, Mayfair Fabrics; Thomas Ashkinaze, Ashkinaze's Men's Styles; and Bernzar Berents, B & D Butchers.

They ask the board not to get rid of going businesses, which pay taxes. "We cannot find anything in the area," Berents said. He's the spokesman. "It would be tragic to eliminate going concerns."

The army spokeswoman, Major Barbara Geddings, said, "We will have to eliminate our youth program at a time when the city's juvenile delinquency rate is growing. This is a part of the city where young people are without parks, without recreation of any kind."

Berents also told the board, which must issue a zoning change before the community center can be built: "We are taxpayers, contributing to the city treasury. What sense does it make to remove us from the city tax base and in our place put a tax-exempt operation? You are finding out that downtown businesses are fleeing every week and your tax base is eroding."

Asked by Harry Kempe, a member of the board, whether the merchants have investigated moving to the mall, Berents said that the merchants have done so but have not been assured of a date when it will be completed.

"We can't just close up and wait," Berents said. "For all we know, the mall won't be built for another two years. What will we do in the meantime? Go on welfare?"

F. Psychiatrist

Your city editor shows you a letter to the editor from Raymond Hertell, chief of psychiatry at the local Whitney-Painter Clinic, one of the most prestigious psychiatric institutions in the country for research and treatment of emotional problems. Dr. Hertell is also head of the state chapter of the American Association of Psychoanalysts.

"See if Dr. Hertell would mind if we run this as a news story. If he doesn't, you might ask him some questions."

The letter reads:

Dear Editor:

I am writing about your recent news article about the Unifying Church members on the college campus.

Is the popularity of the church a bizarre aberration or an age-appropriate response to an adolescent developmental crisis? The church fosters a repudiation of parental ties, a most appealing proposition to the average teenager who is struggling into adulthood.

Simultaneously, the organization functions in loco parentis, demanding complete obedience to norms established by older group members who shepherd the initiates through a series of membership rites.

Strict rules of conduct are established. Monastic asceticism on a quasi-intellectual basis is a lifestyle consistent with the usual adolescent coping mechanisms. The alarm over the church's brainwashing and programming techniques may be excessive. The teenagers' response is consistent with other counter-culture manifestations.

Raymond Hertell, M.D.
Chief of Psychiatry
Whitney-Painter Clinic

You ask Dr. Hertell if his clinic or he personally has treated any young men or women who were with the church or who joined it. He says he has not, but that he has closely followed it from the press accounts.

The editor suggests you write 200–250 words.

Part 2 **Reporting**

Finding Information and Gathering Facts

Skill Drill I: Quality

Certain kinds of data can be used to indicate the quality of life that exists among some groups of people or in certain areas. Here are some figures selected from a recent edition of the *Statistical Abstract of the United States*. The states with the highest and lowest figures are listed below.

1. Write a story based on this listing.
2. Consult the latest edition of the *Statistical Abstract* for your state's standings in the categories listed below and write a story on where your state stands in relation to the top and bottom of the lists.
3. If you notice any other listings you consider important to determining quality of life, take them to class for discussion.

Category	Top	Bottom
Wealth (annual income per capita)	Alaska $7,141	Mississippi $3,677
Homes with full plumbing	Nevada California 99.6%	Alaska 88.3%
Percent of illiteracy	Iowa South Dakota .5%	Louisiana 2.8%
Median years of school completed	Utah Colorado 12.8	Kentucky South Carolina West Virginia 12.1
Expenditure per pupil	Alaska $4,592	Kentucky $1,131
Teacher salaries	Alaska $28,900	New Hampshire $12,900

Doctors per 100,000 population	New York	South Dakota
	261	102
Infant mortality rate (per 1,000 live births)	Delaware	West Virginia
	9.9 (whites)	14.9 (whites)
	Wisconsin	Rhode Island
	15.2 (blacks)	35.2 (blacks)
Suicide rate (per 100,000 population)	Nevada	New Jersey
	24.8	7.2
Death rate from cirrhosis of the liver (per 100,000 population)	New York	Hawaii
	19.9	6.7
Divorce and annulments per 100,000 population	Nevada	Massachusetts
	16.8	3.0
Life insurance per family	Delaware	Arkansas
	$59,600	$28,300

Skill Drill II: References

What reference works would you consult to obtain the following information:

A. The name of the senior U.S. senator from Nevada.
B. Background about a corporation president.
C. The name of the author of a book published last year.
D. The National FBI crime figures for each of the past five years.
E. Background for an article on professional sports as a big business.
F. A good quote from "Hamlet" to start a story on the local little theater's production of the play.
G. An explanation of how the steam engine developed.
H. The names of all African countries.
I. The names of cities in the U.S. with populations of more than one million.
J. The vote for president in the past 10 elections in three neighboring states.
K. The occupation of a man, while a local resident, who left town five years ago.
L. The states and the zip codes of cities in the country named Mt. Pleasant.
M. Details about the toxic waste problem—the Love Canal disaster—near Buffalo, N.Y., a few years ago.
N. The content of any bills introduced in the last session of the state legislature regulating optometrists.
O. The highway distance between the state capital and Washington, D.C.

Skill Drill III: Arithmetic

Arithmetic is a useful tool in reporting and writing. When tax revenues increase from $1,653,000 to $1,812,000, the reporter who can do percentages can state in his or her lead that tax collections jumped 10 percent. The reporter unable to use this useful tool must be content with an array of figures that will not tell the reader at a glance the extent of the increase. Reporters often have to compute percentages, fractions and rates. The figures below were all supplied by sources. The reporters did the computing. Try your hand.

Percentages

A. The number of bankruptcy cases went from 1,300 to 1,600 in a year. This is an increase of

_____ percent.

B. In the city, arrests increased by _____ percent. Police said last year that there were 18,725 arrests, and in the preceding year the total was 15,025.

C. Her weight ballooned from 145 to 265 pounds while she was visiting her grandmother, a _____ percent increase.

D. The faculty contributions reached $1,450 this year, a _____ percent increase over the $1,050 donated last year.

E. The average textbook now runs about 200 pages, he said, compared to about 350 a decade ago.

Today's texts are _____ percent of the size of those 10 years ago, but the price has gone up about 100 percent.

Fractions

A. During the Depression, milk consumption by children was _____ of what it had been previously, going from 15 quarts a month to four.

B. About a _____ of the students had grades of B or better, and a _____ failed. Of the 850 students, 265 had A's and B's and 165 failed.

C. _____ times as many children were in the school lunch program last year as five years ago, she said. Last year, there were 1,390, and five years ago, around 450.

D. The United Fund Drive is _____ of the way home, having raised $59,000 toward its $80,000 goal.

E. If any more than a _____ of the felonies were prosecuted as felonies, the courts would be overwhelmed. There were 16,700 felony arrests, and officials estimate the criminal courts can handle up to 1,500 cases a year without breaking down.

Rates

A. If the state were to put $1 million of its surplus in 8-percent government bonds, it would realize a

return of $ _____ a year.

B. The power company said its rate of return under the new rate structure would not be as high as its critics fear. Actually, the new rates are projected to earn $500,000 a year on a total plant

investment of $5,500,000, which would be _____ percent rate of return.

C. He said he chose the new savings bank for its higher rate of interest. The old bank gave him 6 percent on his $60,000 in deposits, or $3,600 a year. The bank he chose pays 6.5 percent and

would return $ _____ a year.

D. The city hopes to sell the $2,000,000 auditorium-construction bond issue at an interest rate of no more than 7 percent, but some officials say it would be more likely to go at 7.5 percent, which would

mean $ _____ a year more in interest payments over the 20-year life of the bonds, or

$ _____ more in interest over the life of the bond issue.

E. Police said the vehicle was seen at the Freeport toll station at 10:15 p.m., and at 10:45 p.m. it passed through the Roxborough exit, 47 miles away. That means the vehicle was averaging

_____ miles an hour on the throughway.

Skill Drill IV: Famous Works

Who wrote, painted, composed, or otherwise created or devised the following?

1. The Republic
2. The Iliad
3. Measure for Measure
4. War and Peace
5. Ulysses (Novel)
6. Under Milk Wood
7. The Waste Land
8. A Hard Day's Night
9. A Doll's House
10. Kubla Khan
11. Miss Lonelyhearts
12. The Aeneid
13. Catcher in the Rye
14. Lord of the Rings
15. Citizen Kane
16. The Brothers Karamazov
17. Eroica Symphony
18. The Magic Flute
19. La Traviata
20. La Dolce Vita
21. The Night of the Iguana
22. The Return of the Native
23. The Decline of the West
24. The Great Gatsby
25. The Magic Mountain
26. Pride and Prejudice
27. La Mer
28. The Sound and the Fury
29. The Sun Also Rises
30. Sister Carrie
31. The Cherry Orchard
32. Candide
33. The Scarlet Letter
34. Wuthering Heights
35. The Mikado
36. Bartleby, the Scrivener
37. Winesburg, Ohio
38. Leaves of Grass
39. On the Origin of the Species
40. Bleak House
41. Of Human Bondage
42. The Turn of the Screw
43. The Stranger
44. To His Coy Mistress
45. Through the Looking-Glass
46. Don Quixote
47. Madame Bovary
48. Mona Lisa
49. Guernica
50. Birth of a Nation
51. Mein Kampf
52. USA
53. Ten Little Indians
54. La Belle Dame Sans Merci
55. Catch-22
56. Tom Jones
57. Richard III
58. Lysistrata
59. The Emperor Jones
60. Walden
61. The Model T
62. The Interpretation of Dreams
63. The Education of Henry Adams
64. Die Meistersinger
65. Sonnets from the Portuguese
66. Faust
67. The Gettysburg Address
68. The Faerie Queene
69. Das Kapital
70. The Steam Engine
71. Swan Lake
72. The Metamorphosis
73. First Epistle to Corinthians
74. Symphonie Fantastiqué
75. Swann's Way
76. The Shame of the Cities
77. Essay Concerning Human Understanding
78. Germinal
79. The 95 Theses
80. Black Boy
81. The Trout Quintet
82. Nichomachean Ethics
83. The City of God
84. Le Sacre du Printemps
85. Discourse on Method
86. Death in the Afternoon
87. Time Magazine
88. The Cotton Gin
89. Pygmalion
90. Sons and Lovers
91. Point Counter Point
92. Coming of Age in Samoa
93. The Studs Lonigan Trilogy
94. Grapes of Wrath
95. The Sermon on the Mount
96. Ivanhoe
97. The Jungle
98. Jane Eyre
99. The Wealth of Nations
100. Fidelio

Exercise

A. Growth

The news office at Mallory College has released some figures for the current academic year and for 10 years ago:

	Now	10 Years Ago
Students	1,608	1,435
Faculty	118	105
Holding doctorates	86	52
Buildings	40	33
Volumes in Library	325,000	245,000
Annual Operating Budget	$9,709,000	$4,695,000
Endowment		
Book Value	$25,937,156	$11,770,500
Market Value	$28,732,939	$14,888,675
Investment in Plant	$17,348,159	$11,274,100
Total Assets	$47,882,229	$25,711,500
Faculty Salary Scales		
Instructor	$9,450–12,500	$6,000–9,000
Assistant professor	$11,000–18,100	$7,000–12,000
Associate professor	$16,000–21,850	$8,500–15,000
Full professor	$18,900–30,700	$11,000–19,000
Student Aid		
Number Assisted	460	348
Total Awards	$1,179,000	$650,000

The college president, Robert L. Walker, described it as "a decade of progress," according to the press release accompanying the data. The release goes on, quoting Walker:

> In every category, there is marked improvement. We have finally, through the addition of our science center, been able to improve our offerings in the physical sciences. Our library has grown considerably.
>
> But it would be dangerous to rest on this growth. We are faced with ever-increasing demands on our plant. Our faculty salaries are not competitive with other small, high-quality liberal arts schools. We need more money for student aid to match our tuition increase from $2,000 ten years ago to $4,000 today.
>
> I think that our first priority will have to be to raise funds for a library addition. I foresee a fund drive of $4,500,000.
>
> This will be one of our major construction projects. . . .

Your editor suggests that in addition to using some of the data you make calculations of your own to derive relevant information. Write 350 words.

5 How Reporters Work

Exercises

A. Ignorance

You are thumbing through a magazine and you come across a familiar name, Jorge Luis Borges. He is an Argentine writer who visited the local college, Mallory, on a national tour of five colleges last year. On his return to Argentina, he made a statement from which the magazine quotes. This is the quote that catches your eye:

> American college students are extraordinarily ignorant. They read only what they must to pass or what the professors choose. Otherwise, they are totally dedicated to television, to baseball and football.
>
> The United States has lost the literary tradition that produced such writers as Emerson, Thoreau, Melville and Frost.

You check the clips and find a brief story about his speaking to English classes at Mallory. You then call the English department and the chairman, Justin McCarthy, tells you the department was the host for Sr. Borges' visit. In answer to your question about the writer's reactions, he says:

> Yes, I saw the article containing that material. Like all generalizations, there is truth and untruth in it.
>
> But I tend to agree. I've been teaching here and elsewhere in colleges for 28 years and clearly students are not as well read today as their parents were.
>
> Class discussions are not as lively. Sometimes you feel as though you are striking a hollow object. All you hear is your own thumping.
>
> You know, I find something fascinating happening now in the written work I receive. The imagery is from television characters. Whereas we used to have references to the Bible, Shakespeare and mythology, or characters in fairy tales or from Hemingway, we now have these television personalities.
>
> As someone who doesn't look at television, I'm unable to cope with these compositions.

You ask what he predicts in the long run. He answers:

> Each year, we go into class hoping it will be different. But I'm not a pessimist. It may be wishful thinking, but I have to think we will return to our tradition of Emerson, Thoreau and the other great writers of our past.

Write 250–300 words.

B. Acne

Assume the following article is from a recent issue of the *Journal of the American Medical Association*. Summarize in a paragraph of no more than three sentences of your own language the purpose and conclusion of the article. Then write a story of 350–400 words.

Note: As a conscientious reporter, you wonder about the sponsorship of the study, which is mentioned in small type at the end of the article. Your editor suggests you write to the foundation that made the grant and ask if it has any connection with the chocolate manufacturing industry. You receive a letter from F. L. Handy, administrative assistant, who states:

> In response to your recent inquiry, the John A. Hartford Foundation, Inc., has no connection with the chocolate industry.
>
> The foundation was established in 1929 by John A. Hartford and incorporated in New York State in 1932. Its capital funds came from bequests by John A. Hartford and his brother, George L., both deceased, whose father founded the Great Atlantic & Pacific Tea Co.
>
> The foundation's area of interest is biochemical research conducted mainly in medical schools and teaching hospitals.
>
> Among some 300 medical research projects currently being funded is one at the Hospital of the University of Pennsylvania for a study of the causes and treatment of acne, being directed by an eminent dermatologist. His investigations are wide ranging and, among other things, he once sought to determine whether chocolate was indeed a causative factor. But may we assure you that this was but a small and passing phase in several years of sophisticated biochemical studies that have contributed much new medical knowledge on the etiology of acne and a new clinically tested treatment which is the most effective of any developed to date. For a brief report on this see the item on page 2 of the enclosed bulletin.

Here is the article. It is by James E. Fulton, Jr., M.D.; Gerd Plewig, M.D.; and Albert M. Kligman, M.D., Ph.D., members of the Department of Dermatology, University of Pennsylvania School of Medicine, Philadelphia.

Effect of Chocolate on Acne Vulgaris

To test the widespread idea that chocolate is harmful in instances of acne vulgaris, 65 subjects with moderate acne ate either a bar containing ten times the amount of chocolate in a typical bar or an identical-appearing bar which contained no chocolate. Counting of all the lesions on one side of the face before and after each ingestion period indicated no difference between the bars. Five normal subjects ingested two enriched chocolate bars daily for one month; this represented a daily addition of the diet of 1,200 calories, of which about half was vegetable fat. This excessive intake of chocolate and fat did not alter the composition or output of sebum. A review of studies purporting to show that diets high in carbohydrate or fat stimulate sebaceous secretion and adversely affect acne vulgaris indicates that these claims are unproved.

Throughout history, foods have been reviled or favored in accordance with whether they were thought to be baleful or beneficial in disease. The strength of these beliefs has been proportionate to ignorance regarding etiology. Some recondite psychology has decreed that in serious, killing diseases, special foods tend to be prescribed, whereas in lesser afflictions, proscription is the rule. Acne vulgaris is a sovereign example of the latter. No foods are favored for acne victims, but many are inveighed against with holy furor. The list of forbidden foods has one remarkable feature: all of the blacklisted items are delicious and delectable to the adolescent taste. High on the list are such desiderata as nuts, candy, carbonated beverages, shellfish, cheese, and malted milk. While certain of these are deprecated more than others, none is more universally condemned than chocolate. It is a rare general practitioner and an odd dermatologist who is not persuaded that chocolate aggravates acne. We could find but one publication, from Missouri, which following the skeptical traditions of that state, questions the harmfulness of chocolate.

The prevalent beliefs concerning the influence of chocolate or any foodstuff on acne are no more than personal credos which cannot be put before the scientific assembly for evaluation. Controlled investigation is entirely lacking.

Whether foods influence acne is a matter of prime importance in theory and in practice. The disease is enough of a curse without gustatory deprivation.. Moreover, if a food can really alter a disease, when there is no metabolic or nutritional deficiency, that finding alone would set into motion a wholesale attack on the effects of foods on normal physiologic functions.

We decided therefore to undertake a controlled investigation of the effect of chocolate on the course of acne vulgaris.

Materials and Methods

Clinical Evaluation.—The study commenced with 71 subjects, of whom 65 completed the test. The subjects were drawn from two populations: (1) 30 adolescents (14 girls and 16 boys) attending a special acne clinic at the University Hospital, Philadelphia, and (2) 35 young adult male prisoner volunteers. Most of the subjects believed that chocolate was bad for acne. Some "knew" with certainty that eating a chocolate bar a day would be disastrous. Whites predominated in both groups.

Attempts were made to minimize error by incorporating the following controls.

1. Only subjects with mild to moderate acne were included, so as to enhance the possibility of detecting worsening. The clinical state was evaluated by counting all the comedones, papules, and pustules on the left side of the face, on a weekly basis, at the beginning, middle, and end of the test period. A bland, nonmedicated lotion was the sole treatment.

2. A blind study was made possible through the Chocolate Manufacturers Association of the USA. Two bars, a control bar (A), and an enriched chocolate bar (B), identical in size, shape, color, and wrapping were supplied. To our astonishment, these were remarkably similar in taste, although the control bar contained no chocolate. The composition of these bars and, for comparison, that of an ordinary 10-cent bar of milk chocolate is shown in Table 1. The test bars were quite similar with respect to calories and percentage of fat. Both weighed 112 to 114 gm; bar A contained slightly more calories, 592 compared with 557 for bar B. The placebo bar A contained 28% vegetable fat to mimic the lipids contained in chocolate liquor and cocoa butter. Bar B was of bittersweet chocolate.

We deliberately contrived to have the subjects ingest high quantities of chocolate daily, greatly in excess of what is likely to be consumed by even the passionate lover of chocolate. Bar B actually contained more than ten times the amount of chocolate liquor of a typical 10-cent milk chocolate bar weighing 45 gm.

3. A crossover, single-blind format was followed. The subjects ate one bar of either A or B type once daily for four weeks and, after a three-week rest period, the alternate bar for another month. To simplify interpretation, a subject was considered worse, if the lesion count increased 30% at the end of a test period; improved, if lesion count decreased 30%; and unaffected, if there was less than a 30% change. Complaints of gastrointestinal discomfort were common but irregular with both bars. Five subjects gave this discomfort as the reason for quitting the test.

Measuring the Effect of Excessive Chocolate Ingestion.—Five healthy, adult male prisoners volunteered for this portion of the study. Each ingested two of the bittersweet chocolate bars daily for one month. It is reemphasized that this amounts to 20 times more chocolate liquor than is contained in a 10-cent bar of milk chocolate. The volunteers ate the regular prison diet ad lib. Four of the five gained 2.3 to 4.5 kg (5 to 10 lb) during the test period.

Sebum Production.—Sebum production was assayed by the method of Strauss and Pochi, in which sebum is collected in cigarette papers fastened to the forehead for three hours. Sebum output was determined on three consecutive days before the test period; on two consecutive days midway; and on days 30, 31, and 32 at the end.

Sebum Composition.—The composition of sebum was determined by photodensitometric thin-layer chromatography at the beginning of the study, after two weeks, at the end, and 14 days after ingestion of the bars. Sebum was collected in the morning, before the prisoners washed, by placing 10 ml of redistilled ethyl ether in a glass cup and holding it to the cheek for two minutes. The samples were shipped in aluminum-capped glass tubes to the laboratory of Don Downing, Ph.D, in Boston, who performed the sebum analysis. Rubber and plastic caps could not be used, since ether extracts contaminating compounds.

Comedogenic Potency.—Comedogenic potency was assayed in the external ear canal of the rabbit after the method of Kligman and Katz. Scalp sebum was collected before and after the ingestion period by having each subject dip his head into a basin of ethyl ether on three consecutive days. After volatilization, the residue was inuncted into the rabbit ear canal once daily, five days a week, for two weeks. The amount of comedo formation was assessed at the end of this time, from horizontally sectioned biopsies.

Results

Clinical.—The results are summarized in the Figure. With the bittersweet chocolate bar, the conditions of 46 of the 65 subjects remained the same, 10 were better, and 9 worse. With the control bar, conditions of 53 remained the same, 5 were better, and 7 worsened. These differences are insignificant, though it is hard to resist pointing out that conditions of twice as many subjects improved after they had eaten chocolate. The adolescent patients and the slightly older prisoners did not materially differ in their responses; hence, the data are not further subdivided. After a rest period of two months, four of the inmates who had previously experienced acne flare-ups after eating chocolate were given the bittersweet chocolate bar again. One defected at the end of two weeks because of gastrointestinal upset. However, in no case did the acne flare again.

Effect on Sebum of Ingesting Two Enriched Chocolate Bars Daily.—Sebum Production.—Table 2 summarizes the average sebum production for each of the five subjects at the beginning of the study, at two weeks, and after one month. No clear trend is discernible. In three there was an apparent increase, and in two an apparent decrease. Although the sample size is small and the method imprecise, it seems likely that forced feeding of chocolate does not importantly affect the output of sebum.

Sebum Composition.—The effect on the major lipid fractions of sebum is shown in Table 3. Again, no trend is discernible. Throughout, the values for the fatty acids tend to be higher than usual. Downing suggests that this results from continued lipolysis during transit of the specimens. However, the sum of the glycerides and free fatty acids is in the usual range. It is well known that there is an inverse relationship between the two, as must be the case since the fatty acids derive hydrolytically from the glycerides. Although excessive chocolate consumption did not affect the general composition of sebum, we cannot categorically assert that there was no change, since individual fatty acids were not assayed.

Comedogenic Potency.—The sebum of all five subjects was moderately to strongly comedogenic before treatment. This did not change after the ingestion of chocolate. This is consistent with the lack of chemical change of the sebum.

Comment

The key finding in this study can be reduced to a simple statement: ingestion of high amounts of chocolate did not materially affect the course of acne vulgaris or the output or composition of sebum. Actually, since the bittersweet bars contain about one third fat, we may also infer that a diet rich in vegetable fat probably does not alter sebaceous secretion. The literature on the effect of dietary fats and carbohydrates on acne and sebaceous secretion is singularly confusing, contradictory, and controversial. Yet the belief that foods adversely influence skin disease is ancient and deeply rooted. More proofs than we have supplied will doubtless be necessary before long-held clinical prejudices will yield gracefully to experimentation.

In reviewing an extensive experimental literature, mainly about animals, one becomes keenly aware of a remarkably consistent outcome. It is almost always found that high fat or carbohydrate levels increase either the quantity or quality of lipids excreted by the skin. If true, this would provide a plausible explanation for the exacerbating effects of such diets. For example, forced feeding of fats has not only been found to increase sebaceous output, but—perhaps even more remarkable—the fed lipid was excreted unchanged. Somekawa's observations on rats fed whale oil are perhaps typical of the wish to believe that high-fat diets affect lipid excretion. While there is no doubt that the skin of these animals dripped with oil, this was clearly not due to excretion via the skin, but to the spreading out of unabsorbed oil from the anus.

Another experimental limitation relates to the difficulty of accurately determining sebum output in hairy animals. Investigators who found increases in sebaceous secretion after fat feeding usually did not take the trouble to establish the reliability of their methods. Such a criticism applies notably to the oft-quoted work of Suzuki who, with excessive feeding of fats to rabbits, obtained increase of 70% to 111% of sebaceous secretion in two weeks. As a matter of fact, there has been only one critical study of the influence of dietary fats, and the conclusion clearly refutes the prevailing dogma. Nikkari fed rats diets containing 20% stearic, oleic, or linoleic acids, or cholesterol. He measured sebum output by collecting the total surface lipids four days after a previous removal of the fats, and analyzed the components by chemical and chromatographic methods. Neither the quality nor quantity of the surface lipids was affected. Nikkari states categorically that the sebaceous glands cannot serve as an excretory pathway for lipids. When C stearate was given, only a tiny fraction (0.4%) of the radioactivity appeared in the sebum, and this was no longer present as stearate but had been incorporated in all major lipid fractions of sebum.

Similarly, those who experiment on humans generally find that diet may change the amount and composition of the lipids excreted. Serrati found increases in forehead lipids when either excess carbohydrates or fats were given. MacDonald gave healthy men a low-fat diet, augmented either with 500 gm a day of starch or sucrose, for 25 days. Both caused some increase in the straight-chain C monounsaturated fatty acid; only starch increased the saturated C acid. He also gave 28 gm/kg of chocolate to 29 adolescents for five days. This increased the cholesterol content of the surface lipids, and the triglyceride in the surface lipids diminished in men, but not in women!

Lipkin et al have begun to attack the problem of finding out whether fats can pass unchanged from the blood via the sebaceous gland to the surface of the body. They perfused radioactive palmitic acid, triolein, cholesterol, and cholesteryl esters through a skin flap in dogs. Less than 1% of each of these substances could be recovered from the anatomical portion representing the epidermis and sebaceous glands. This is hardly conclusive and probably reflects contamination, since much higher amounts were found in underlying dermis.

The question is not whether circulating substances such as drugs can enter the gland; they almost certainly can. We have found that tetracycline reaches the body surface partly via sebum. The key point is whether circulating lipids can be excreted without being metabolized. We think not.

One must be cautioned not to compare sebaceous gland to adipose tissue. This latter is essentially a fat-storing, not a fat-elaborating, organ. The lipids of the subcutaneous tissue are vastly simpler: more than 99% is triglyceride, practically all of which is accounted for by a few fatty acids. Excess dietary fats unquestionably do alter the composition of subcutaneous fat after prolonged intake. Thus, with a diet rich in corn oil, the adipose lipids may slowly come to resemble corn oil.

On the other hand, there is considerable circumstantial evidence that blood lipids are not excreted by the sebaceous glands. The likelihood is that these are hydrolized to simple carbon fragments from which all the multifarious sebaceous lipids are synthesized by the gland. If this were not so, the lipids present in serum would also occur in sebum. There are a number of ready examples to show that such is not the case. For instance, the unsaturated C fatty acid in sebum is not linoleic, as in serum. Of the 18:1 fatty acid in serum, more than 95% is $\Delta°$, whereas in sebum 20% is $\Delta°$. All of the 16:1 acid in serum is $\Delta°$ and all in sebum is $\Delta°$, as noted by Don Downing, PhD (written communication Feb. 8, 1969). An even more extraordinary case in point is that in animal species, the sebum contains little or no triglycerides, though these are abundant in the serum.

As regards clinical studies of the influence of diet on acne, perhaps, the less said the better. An egregious example of unwarranted assertions is afforded by Hoehn's tract, "Acne and Diet." Although we do not know the true prevalence of acne in any land, Hoehn compared supposedly low-incidence countries such as Korea, Spain, Turkey, and Eskimo villages where the principal source of fats is vegetable oils, fish, and fowl, with high-incidence locations like Pakistan, the United States, and Mombasa,

Kenya, where the main source is saturated animal fat. Thus furnished with data as wide as the world itself, Hoehn instituted a diet low in unsaturated vegetable fat, avoiding animal fats. Not unexpectedly, the beneficial effects in instances of acne were dramatic.

Though much more critical work is required, present knowledge suggests that the sebaceous gland has a high degree of autonomy. Neither the intensity nor quality of its activity is very sensitive to the internal or external milieu. The principle of homeostasis doubtlessly applies to tissues as well as to fluids. It would be remarkable if skin functions were easily influenced by the vagaries of the diverse diets which have evolved in human populations.

This investigation was supported by a grant from the John A. Hartford Foundation.

Skill Drill: Auditing Your Emotions

Reporters, like everyone else, have feelings that influence the way they see the world. Sometimes these emotional responses obstruct observation. You might aduit your feelings by checking the boxes below and then matching your responses with those of other students.

	Positive	Neutral	Negative
American Legion	☐	☐	☐
Bartenders	☐	☐	☐
Bill of Rights	☐	☐	☐
Bird Watchers	☐	☐	☐
Black Muslims	☐	☐	☐
Capitalism	☐	☐	☐
Communism	☐	☐	☐
Daughters of the American Revolution (DAR)	☐	☐	☐
The Elderly	☐	☐	☐
The Flag	☐	☐	☐
Football Players	☐	☐	☐
Free Enterprise	☐	☐	☐
Girl Scouts	☐	☐	☐
Go-go Dancers	☐	☐	☐
Homosexuals	☐	☐	☐
Housewives	☐	☐	☐

	Positive	Neutral	Negative
Jazz	☐	☐	☐
Ku Klux Klan	☐	☐	☐
Labor Unions	☐	☐	☐
The Mafia	☐	☐	☐
Opera	☐	☐	☐
Park Rangers	☐	☐	☐
Pentecostal Churches	☐	☐	☐
Plastic Surgeons	☐	☐	☐
Policemen	☐	☐	☐
Puerto Ricans	☐	☐	☐
Radicals	☐	☐	☐
Republicans	☐	☐	☐
The Roman Catholic Church	☐	☐	☐
The Rotary Club	☐	☐	☐
Scandanavians	☐	☐	☐
Science Fiction	☐	☐	☐
Sierra Club	☐	☐	☐
Socialism	☐	☐	☐
Southerners	☐	☐	☐
Truck Drivers	☐	☐	☐
The United Nations	☐	☐	☐
Wall Street	☐	☐	☐
Youth	☐	☐	☐
Zionism	☐	☐	☐

6 Planning the Story

Exercises

A. Goals

A well-known British literary critic who also appears on television (BBC) is giving the major address at the annual state convention of the Daily Newspaper Association, which is held in conjunction with Newspaper Day on the local campus. The speaker is Jeffrey St. George. His topic is: "Goals for Journalism Education." He will speak at 8 o'clock tonight. Here are some excerpts supplied by the campus press office from the text of his talk which you should use for a story of 300–350 words.

> Your experiences in this country with public events and public officials have served to develop a sense of responsibility and maturity in your press that is, I believe, unmatched anywhere in the world. This is a positive development for educators who prepare men and women for newspapers and stations. Let us try to set out some goals for the journalism educator so that he or she may respond to these needs.
>
> Clearly, a professional education must give the student skills and a sense of craft. But it is not enough to prepare the student only for his first job. The education must be sufficiently broad and deep so that the underpinnings of a creative and positive life are established. There must be established a commitment to the contemplative as well as the active life, for skills without understanding become as automatic as the water pump. . . .
>
> I do not mean to imply that these aims are visionary. Journalism education in your country is clearly moving in this direction. I should only wish to reinforce the movement. I would suggest a few questions any educator might ask of the program of study he or she is adopting:
>
> > Will the curriculum or the course do the following:
> > —Will it give the student a sense of purpose and broaden his knowledge?
> > —Will it deepen his interest in ideas, give him sufficient materials to think about?
> > —Will it free the imagination and develop initiative?
> > Finally, the fourth question whose answer might be the most important of all of these:
> > —Will it develop a free and open mind, a journalist free of biases of his society so that he can act independently, intelligently and spontaneously?
>
> In closing, let me emphasize that I do not share the disdain of some educators for the real needs of the editor for young reporters who can spell words of their mother tongue correctly and who can use a comma and a period with precision. But I do believe that this can hardly be the goal of journalism education. Nor, for that matter, can the education be narrowly conceived as instruction in the forms and practices of current journalism, which is only a step beyond the rules of grammar, punctuation and spelling. All are essential, of course. To use the words of one of my countrymen, Alfred North Whitehead, "The major aim of education should be an understanding of the insistent present."

B. Wedding

You are the courthouse reporter for an Albuquerque newspaper and come across this suit among a dozen on file. Write 150–200 words. (Mr. and Mrs. Lopez live at 712 Silver Ave., SW.)

STATE OF NEW MEXICO   COUNTY OF BERNALILLO

                 IN THE SECOND JUDICIAL DISTRICT COURT

TOBIAS LOPEZ and   )
CAROLYN LOPEZ,   )
his wife,   )
            Plaintiffs,   )
)
     -vs-   )
)
MRS. L. DURRANCE and   )   No._____578749_____
THE WOMEN'S CLUB, INC.,   )
)   FILED IN MY OFFICE THIS
            Defendants.   )
)   AUG 12
_____)

                                      Solomon Gallegos

                    COMPLAINT   CLERK DISTRICT COURT

          Plaintiffs state:

                              I

          That on or about 8 July 1976 Plaintiffs entered into a

lease contract with Defendants for the purpose of leasing premises

known as Women's Club Hall at 22 Gold Avenue, SW, for a wedding

celebration to take place between the hours of 8:00 p.m. and 12:00

p.m., on 25 July 1976.

                             II

          That rental was paid therefor and accepted by Defendants.

                            III

          That as a result of said agreement, Plaintiffs invited

over 200 parties for said wedding celebration, relied upon said

agreement therefor, made large and elaborate preparation, including

the hiring of musical entertainment therefor, and planned a

honeymoon trip immediately after the culmination of said celebration,

all with knowledge to invitees and said Defendants.

IV

That on 25 July 1976 at the hour of 8:00 p.m. Plaintiffs,
together with approximately 200 invitees, and their orchestra,
attempted to enter said premises as per their contract and were met
by another party of approximately 100 people who advised Plaintiffs
and their invitees that said hall was being used by them and that
Plaintiffs and their invitees could not use said hall for the
purpose for which Defendants promised.

V

That the entire wedding celebration was ruined, all to
the deep and everlasting and irreparable humiliation suffered by
Plaintiffs and their invitees.

VI

That as a result of the ruination of said celebration,
the humiliation suffered by Plaintiffs, the gross embarrassment
to their reputation, Plaintiffs were forced to postpone perhaps
indefinitely their honeymoon trip, Plaintiff CAROLYN LOPEZ suffered
deep and excruciating shock to her nervous system, the
extent of which is unknown to Plaintiffs.

WHEREFORE, Plaintiffs pray for judgment against
Defendants, and each of them, in the sum of Five Thousand ($5,000.00)
Dollars plus costs herein lawfully expended.

7 Rudiments of the News Story

Skill Drills: Guidelines

Each of the following items violates at least one of the basic guidelines for writing news stories. The guidelines are:

> **Accuracy** in detail and expression.
> **Attribution** of all statements and information to reliable sources.
> **Verification** of assertions, charges.

Balance and **fairness.**
Brevity.
Human interest in stories when possible.
News point stressed.

Identify the errors. When possible, make corrections or indicate what should be done.

A. Salary

He said his take-home pay from his salary of $150 a week as an elevator operator was slightly more than $100 a week. His weekly deductions included: social security, $6; federal taxes, $36; and state taxes, $11. (Paragraph in story.)

B. Fine

He was fined $25 last year for loitering near the theater. But his felony conviction did not deter him from his task. (Paragraph in story.)

C. Resignation

Jenkins announced his resignation yesterday. He is quitting the force because of its authoritarian structure and the dictatorial attitude of Chief McCabe. (Paragraph in story.)

D. Shots

A city plan, proposed by municipal health authorities today, would inoculate all unleashed animals and take them to the local pound where they would be given anti-rabies shots and returned to their owners after a $15 fine is paid. (Lead.)

E. Success

Lee capped his successful 1975 season with the Red Sox by helping his teammates to win the World Series against the Cincinatti Reds, Peralta said in his talk to the Boosters' Club. (Paragraph in story.)

F. Talk

The local chapter of the Public Relations Society said today Jose Lopez Garcia, director of an advertising agency in Mexico City, will address its meeting Oct. 20 at 8 p.m. in the Chamber of Commerce board room.

Mr. Garcia is on a tour of this country to gather ideas for the Mexican public relations industry. (Short item.)

G. Noise

A special airport-sound study committee, set up at the local air field, issued its report, Marshall Peat, airport manager, reported today.

The study was set up to determine whether there would be any noise problems in the area of the field if the undeveloped land to the northeast of the field were developed for use as a housing project.

The report shows frequent complaints and a decline in housing values in the developed area.

"That should kill the housing proposal of Mitchell & Co.," Peat said. "But I'm not sure as they have a lot of money invested in the land." More than 250 acres are involved. Half the residents of the area said they intend to move if they can find housing. (Story.)

H. New Age

"A new age of pot is dawning," said Albert Goldman in his talk to the Rotary Club this afternoon.

Goldman, a writer, said marijuana will replace liquor and tobacco as the new middle-class social habit. Already, he said, it is used by almost all age and social groups. Since it has no known ill effects, Goldman said, it is safer than the habit-forming alcohol and cigarettes. (Story.)

I. Adoption

Robert G. Dowle was named head of the Interfaith Children's Agency today at the annual meeting of the board.

The agency arranges for the adoption of local youngsters through the various religious groups and the city social services department.

Dowle said he was pleased by the appointment, particularly since he was placed in the home of his adoptive parents, Mr. and Mrs. Albert Dowle, in the first year of the agency's operation in 1937. (Story.)

J. Tour

During his travels, he stopped off in Iceland, the world's largest island. He toured the interior, which is covered with an enormous sheet of ice. He said the island was discovered by Eric the Red almost 1,000 years ago. (Part of story.)

Exercises

A. Opening React

A local merchant, Russell Rothkrug, owner of Russ's Market, which is across the street from the campus, calls the city editor with a complaint. The editor turns the call over to you. He says it is a complaint about the new grocery store on the campus about which the newspaper had a story recently.

"No, it's not the story I don't like," says Rothkrug. "It's the college encouraging the kids to compete with private merchants. We have to operate at a profit, but these kids don't have families to support or rent to pay. I think it's unfair."

You ask if his business has been affected.

"Sure it has. Since that store opened 10 days ago my business has fallen off about 20 percent."

Has he done anything?

"Yeah, I called the dean, Thomas Palmer, and complained, but all he would say is that he would look into it. He wasn't very encouraging."

You check with another merchant near the campus, Aaron Elston, owner of A-1 Shopping Center, and he says that he, too, has been disturbed, but that he has not yet noticed any appreciable downturn.

"Maybe 10 percent. But I am worried what it may be like when word spreads around the campus. They certainly don't have any costs, like hiring a guard here to keep those college kids from stealing everything off the shelves.

"They won't do that to the campus store. Well, maybe they will. Maybe those junior businessmen will learn what it's like to be a small merchant. Oh, the worries and the taxes and the ripoffs and the lousy quality of goods. You know, now that I think of it, I hope they stick around for a while. Those kids who talk so much about how private enterprise is exploitative may learn something.

"Tell that kid running the store I'll be happy to give him the name of my doctor. He has some good stuff for the nerves."

Write a story of 300 words.

B. Cab

You work for a daily newspaper in Atlantic City, N.J., and a friend tells you about a couple, Ronald and Marie McHugh, of the nearby town of Brigantine, both in their 50s, who were recently married and took a bus to New York City for a weekend honeymoon. They had problems. You call McHugh, and he tells you this story:

We thought we'd go up to the Big Apple and enjoy a good time. Brigantine isn't exactly the most exciting place for a honeymoon. We had reservations in the Waldorf Astoria and were going to hear Guy Lombardo at the Rainbow Room, which Marie has always wanted to do.

We got a cab outside the Port Authority Bus Terminal. That was Friday night. He took us to the hotel and we got out. I went to the trunk to wait for the driver to get the luggage. He took off. I couldn't believe my eyes. He zoomed off.

We had three new pieces of luggage and Marie's cosmetic bag. And wedding gifts, including two envelopes with $100 cash in each. The doorman told us to take another cab and follow him, but the lights were against us and after about five blocks we lost him.

We got his license and the police called up a couple of days after we got back and told us they went to an apartment and found one suitcase, empty.

We left Saturday morning, maybe the shortest honeymoon on record. This weekend, I think we'll walk the boardwalk or play Monopoly at home. Last weekend was a nightmare.

Write a story for your newspaper.

C. Waiter

A woman, Mrs. Arthur Katzen, 896 Armour Blvd., telephones the newsroom to say she wants to describe a pleasant experience she had in New York City on a recent trip. She had read a piece in your newspaper about a honeymooning couple whose luggage was stolen by a taxi driver on their arrival in New York. She says:

I was staying at the Waldorf Astoria this weekend and had breakfast in the Peacock Alley. I left what I thought was a $1 tip. During the day I noticed that I was short of money and couldn't figure out why.

The next morning I went back for breakfast in the Peacock Alley, a waiter came over to me and handed me a $20 bill. He said I'd left it as a tip.

So you see, not everyone there is a thief. He was such a pleasant young man. I gave him a reward of $5 for returning the $20.

D. Stuck

A court attendant tells you that Judge John Kramer had an unusal case in Civil Court and that the jury has just returned a verdict. He seems unable to control a laugh. You ask him what is funny, and he just points down the corridor to the judge's office. There, you ask the clerk, Bert Schneider, and he tells you:

Great case. The plaintiff is Beulah Wright, 87 West End Ave., the defendant, Intercity Bus Co., of Mount Kisco. She sued for $45,000 damages. Charged that while riding in bus Aug. 14 she went to restroom. The bus swerved and her posterior struck the emergency window, which popped out.

Her posterior was stuck there for several minutes; finally, she managed to pry herself free, after bus driver stopped on hearing her screams.

She complains of severe emotional distress as a result of the embarrassment over the incident.

Jury awarded $4,300 damages.

Oh, yes—she was fully clothed, according to the testimony.

Write a brief story.

E. No Baby

You are looking at some old clips and your eye catches a story about Baby, an African elephant in the local zoo whose pregnancy was reported by the zoo director, Cyrus Tucek, five months ago. You wonder how Baby is faring and you call the zoo.

Tucek is not there but his assistant, Bayard Parker, fills you in with a few words.

"She isn't," he tells you.

"Isn't what?" you ask.

"Pregnant," he replies.

"What happened?" you ask.

"False pregnancy, I guess," he says.

Sensing that Parker is a man of few words, but hoping to draw him out, you say you never heard of such a thing.

"Well, you have now," he says.

"How's she doing generally?" you ask.

"OK."

"When did you find out about Baby's false pregnancy?"

"Two days ago."

"When will Mr. Tucek be back?"

"Two weeks."

You decide you can't wait that long. Anyway, you see that you have the basic information, and you decide to write a short.

F. Hot Line

There have been rumors in Washington, D.C., that the president was awakened by a wrong number that was plugged in on his hot line. This is the closely guarded private wire between the White House and the Pentagon over which the president would first be told of any enemy attack and would give the order that might mean all-out nuclear war.

The White House press secretary confirms the story. He gives out the following facts:

The president happened to be awake late one night recently when the "hot line" buzzed. He picked up the phone and heard a strange voice:

"Is this the animal hospital?"

"No," said the president.

"Is this South 5—6855?"

"No, this is the White House."

"Is Mr. Smathers there?"

"No, this is the president."

The caller disconnected.

At the Animal Hosptial in Alexandria, Va., the switchboard operator tells you, "For the past three weeks we've had trouble with the phone. We've been hearing other conversations. Apparently there have been some crossed wires somewhere."

She says the Chesapeake and Potomac Telephone Co. has been asked to find out how a wrong number could be plugged in on the president's private hot line.

8 Writing the Lead

Skill Drill I: Lead Choice

Indicate whether a direct or a delayed lead would be appropriate for these events.

A. Adoption of the city budget. _____

B. Announcement of a performance next month of "Trial by Jury" by the local Gilbert and Sullivan

   Society. _____

C. Introduction of calculators into grade school arithmetic classes. _____

D. Election of officers of the county medical society. _____

E. Award of fellowship to a faculty member. _____

F. Arrival of Barnum & Bailey Circus in town. _____

G. Preparations of Francie Larrieu for metric-mile race in Olympics. _____

H. Teaching innovations by modern language department. _____

I. Total United States employment for past year. _____

J. Background of candidate for United States Senate. _____

K. Approval by FCC of interstate telephone rate increase. _____

L. Jury verdict. _____

M. Survey of consumer complaints on automobile repairs. _____

N. Arrest of Utah congressman on charge of soliciting for prostitution. _____

O. Curtis Strange drops out of college to become golf pro. _____

Skill Drill II: Simplifying

Some editors demand short leads, under 30 words whenever possible. This requires reporters to stress single-element and summary leads in their stories. Rewrite the following leads, making them single element or summary with fewer than 30 words.

A. The city planning department plans to make repairs this coming summer on Ogden, Johnson and Kentucky Streets at an estimated cost of $18,000, $22,000 and $78,000, respectively, it was announced by City Engineer Kenneth Keenan.

B. After a three-day search, police today reported the arrest of Eileen McGuire, 19, in a Chicago bus depot on a charge of arson in connection with the fire that left Karvette's Department Store a burned-out hulk last week at an estimated loss of $2 million.

C. The state purchasing agent will open bids Dec. 10 for the purchase of electronic equipment for the state university, including calculators for the mathematics department, audiovisual projectors and tape recorders for the modern language department, and installation of an all-electronic newsroom for the school of journalism. The newsroom installation is expected to cost at least $250,000 and will enable students to write and edit copy without typewriters or pencils.

D. A last-quarter scoring spree by Connie Hawkins, the newly arrived forward, enabled the Bullets to erase a seemingly insurmountable 22-point halftime lead by the Warriors in a come-from-behind win 88–87.

E. "The defendant's crime may not have caused physical harm, but the hardship he inflicted on those who trusted him with their savings cannot be ignored," said Judge George Z. Roberts yesterday in sentencing Norris Josephson to a minimum of five years in the state penitentiary on a fraudulent investment scheme that bilked local residents of more than a half million dollars.

F. The weather bureau today offered little hope to corn and wheat growers across a wide belt of Minnesota with a prediction that no rain is foreseen for the next week to relieve the month-long drought that has cut crops by an estimated 5 percent to date.

G. F. W. Walkenhorst, a university regent, said at a meeting of the regents today that the teaching staff at the state university works an average of fewer than 20 hours a week and that unless this is remedied by a larger course load, the state legislature could not be expected to approve the university's current budget request.

H. The Crested Butte Dam burst last night and a wall of water 12 feet high swept through small towns, farms and ranches in eastern Idaho leaving an unknown number of dead and injured and millions of dollars in destruction.

I. In a talk last night to the local press club, Russell Cooper, a political reporter based in Washington, D.C., said that the traditional role of the political reporter has been superseded by modern advertising techniques, which allow a candidate to project an image the candidate desires in "the picture-hungry, simplicity-oriented media that are unwilling or unable to deal with complexities."

J. The use of publicly employed teachers in religious schools has come under constitutional challenge in a suit filed in federal court here today by the National Coalition for Public Education and Religious Liberty (PEARL) in which the organization contends the United States Commission on Education has violated the Constitution by ignoring Supreme Court rulings barring the assignment of public school teachers to religious schools during regular school hours.

 9 Structuring the Story

Discussion: Analysis

The news story structure is:

> **Lead** that contains the most important fact or facts.
> **Body** of the story that contains:
> > Material that amplifies and buttresses the lead.
> > Background information.
> > Secondary facts or information.

Analysis

Clip a local news story from the most recent issue of the newspaper you read and break it down into its basic structure. Here is an example of how you might do it with the use of a lettering system.

The city zoning board yesterday approved the construction of a 10-foot-high chain link fence around the Temple B'nai Shalom cemetery to keep out vandals.	Lead—A
But the board denied the congregation's request for a barbed wire at the top of the fence because the cemetery, at 4400 North Rogers Ave., is in a residential zone.	Amplification of lead—A_1
"The fence is not worth anything to us without the barbed wire," William Gamm, a lawyer for the congregation, said last night.	Amplification of lead—A_2
Mr. Gamm said that young people are using the cemetery as a shortcut to a shopping center and that unless an impenetrable fence is erected graves will be desecrated.	Amplification of lead—A_3
The temple made its request for the fence last month following the discovery by members of the congregation of several overturned grave markers.	Background
In other actions, the zoning board acted on the following requests:	Secondary material
Barry Tobin, 532 East Baltimore St., use of first and second floors as massage parlor—postponed.	Secondary fact—B
Raymond Feeney, 67 Drooman Hill, remove one-story rear addition and erect three-story rear addition—approved.	Secondary fact—C
Daniel Snead, 230 South Patterson Park, use of first floor as private club—disapproved.	Secondary fact—D

Exercise I

Analyze the following story, using the sample analysis above as a model:

A. Bids

Apparent low bids totaling $216,000 were submitted today for the renovation of the former Scott Building, 526 Central Ave., for use by the local police and traffic engineering departments as a garage.

The bids were referred by the city purchasing agent to the city engineer for review.

A total of 41 bids were received for four separate contracts involved in the renovation. The city council had appropriated $350,000 for the renovation project. The city has already spent $432,000 for the purchase of the property.

The board also received bids for the purchase of 15 police vehicles, for the purchase of two pickup trucks for the water department, and for the paving of a portion of Elm Street.

Apparent low bidders for the garage renovation, the amount bid and the number of bidders for each contract were:

—General construction: Hesch Construction Corp., of Albany, $111,958, 13 bidders.
—Heating and ventilation: Brown Plumbing and Heating, Inc., of Clovia, $44,492, 10 bidders.
—Plumbing: J. N. Hunsley Co., of Piedmont, $33,332, eight bidders.
—Electrical work: McCall Electric Co. of Albany, $25,980, 10 bidders.

Freeport Dodge, Inc., the sole bidder in each instance, was awarded three contracts to provide 15 police vehicles for a total cost of $60,237.

Freeport Dodge offered the apparent low bid of $8,400 for two pickup trucks. The only other bid of $9,554 was from Simpson Motors Co.

Wrightson Industries Inc., of South Freeport, submitted the apparent low bid of $67,986 for the improvement of 1,500 feet of Elm Street. The council had appropriated $120,000 for the job. There were five other bidders.

In a final action, E. W. Grimes Co., of Freeport, was awarded $15,605 to contract for fireproofing the city-owned Mohawk Brush Building on Fuller Road.

Exercises II

A. Bus

Here are a reporter's notes based on a call from Jack Nagel, who is the press officer for the state Public Utilities Commission:

> The People's Bus Line, Inc., 1320 East Torrence Ave., owner George W. Hulbert, has filed with the state Public Utilities Commission today a request for permission to operate a route into the downtown area from outlying communities, state PUC chairman Michael McKirdy announced today.
>
> Hulbert seeks state approval to operate an unscheduled Monday through Friday service and asserts in his application that "domestic workers needing to reach downtown for trains to the suburbs where they work are not being served by present bus lines." Protests or supporting witnesses will be heard 28 days from the date of the application, at 3 p.m., in the state Executive Office Building.
>
> Hulbert submitted with his request a petition bearing 65 signatures of local residents. The petition has a preamble reading: "We the undersigned find it costly to reach commuter lines from our section of the community and support the request of George W. Hulbert for unscheduled bus service in our area."

B. Missing

It is 60 minutes to deadline, and the police reporter calls in the following notes for you. Write a story:

> Billy Joe Appel, 4, 801 Second Ave., was located at 12:30 p.m. at the home of Mrs. Bernice McCoy, 320 Manley St., a friend of Alice Kragler, 16, the babysitter. He disappeared from the Appel home around 9 o'clock last night when babysitter said she fell asleep looking at TV. He is the son of Alan and Roberta Appel.
>
> Police said after questioning Miss Kragler this morning, she admitted she had wanted to "get even with the Appels for not letting me have my boyfriend visit me when I was babysitting with Billy Joe."
>
> She said she called her friend, Mrs. McCoy, 20, and asked her to take the kid because she had to return home for an emergency and would pick him up in an hour. When Mrs. McCoy heard the news about the missing child on the radio last night she was too frightened to do anything.
>
> The Appels say they are happy to have their child back and are not going to file charges against Miss Kragler.
>
> Quote from Mrs. Appel:
>
> "Alice is a good girl. She just got upset. Those things happen. She loves Billy Joe and would never let anything happen to him."

The police say a full report will be turned over to juvenile authorities since there was a violation of the law. About 20 volunteers turned out last night to search for the child in the woods near the Appel home where the parents thought he had wandered off to.

C. Calendar

Here is the program of dates, times and events for next month at the Civic Auditorium. The public is invited to all events. Fees, if any, are in parentheses. Write a story.

————5, 7 p.m. "Mao as an Expression of the Chinese Political and Cultural Ethos," John Langley, Far Eastern correspondent of the *Toronto Star*. (Free to members of the Community Events Society; $3 to others.)

————10, 8 p.m. A program of chamber music presented by students of the Oberlin Conservatory of Music. Beethoven, Mozart and Ravel quartets. ($5.)

————15, 1 p.m. "The American Indian as Victim," John Dozier, professor emeritus of ethnology, of Stanford University. Sponsored by Friends of the First Citizens.

————16–20, 1–5 p.m. Exhibition of photographs of nature by the members of the Friends of the Earth.

————22, 7 p.m. Speech by Sen. Edward M. Kennedy of Massachusetts, "Making the Political System Work—A Tribute to Party Workers." Sponsored by the state Democratic Party. ($100-a-plate dinner.)

————24–27, 8 p.m. "Yerma," a play by Federico Garcia Lorca, Directed by Francisco Perez and players from the students and faculty of the University of Florida. In Spanish. ($3.)

D. Daredevil

Write a story based on the following information that you obtained in a check with the state highway patrol:

Had a strange one around midnight last night about 20 miles east of Canton. A 20-year-old short-order cook employed by Leek's Cafe was going home when his car went out of control on a bridge over the tracks of Amtrak. Broke through the guardrail, sailed through the air, hit power lines, and then fell to the tracks, landing upside down. The guy was unhurt, but it took 15 minutes to get him out of the car. His name is Alan Taylor. We booked him for reckless and drunk driving, driving without a license and speeding. A guy following him says he must have hit that bridge at 90. Had a 1976 Chevy that he'd modified.

Kind of miraculous all around. It's a wonder he wasn't electrocuted or killed in the fall. If it'd happened a few minutes before, the east-bound Broadway Limited might have hit him and his car.

E. Outage

On a routine check that you make of the sheriff's office 15 minutes before deadline, you are given the following information by the dispatcher:

We got a call from one of our patrol cars about half an hour ago that a car hit a power pole northwest of town and people in the new housing subdivision out there were without electricity for about 45 minutes. I don't know any more than that. Oh yes—no one was hurt in the accident.

You call the local office of the power and light company and the public information officer tells you:

We have just returned service. It was out from 1:02 to 1:40 p.m. It affected Arden Hills where we have 250 meters, all residences. All of them were out.

Write a brief story based on the information. (Arden Hills is a new subdivision. It was completed last year.)

F. Lifesaver

The local police and fire departments have obtained a print of a 16mm film, "How to Save a Choking Victim: The Heimlich Maneuver," and it will be shown free to the public tomorrow evening at 8 o'clock in the Civic Auditorium. The local chapter of the American Red Cross and other organizations urge their members to attend.

Following is a press release from a distributor. Write a one-page story.

FOR IMMEDIATE RELEASE

NEW FILM—A LIFESAVER

Washington, D.C., July 20, 1975—A new film designed to teach how to reduce significantly the sixth largest cause of accidental death in the United States has been placed in national distribution today by the educational film subsidary of Paramount Pictures, Oxford Films.

The 11 minute, 16 mm color film, "How to Save a Choking Victim: The Heimlich Maneuver," shows the three symptoms of a choking victim and demonstrates a simple four-step lifesaving method developed by Dr. Henry J. Heimlich, director of surgery, Jewish Hospital, Cincinnati.

"When I realized that thousands of accidental deaths are caused by choking and there was no satisfactory method for removing an obstruction from the throat, I turned to my 20 years of experience in esophageal surgery and began to work on a solution," said Heimlich.

The Oxford Film features Dr. Heimlich explaining and performing his technique. The maneuver uses manual pressure directed upward on the diaphragm to generate the necessary pressure in the lungs to expel any obstruction. It can be self-administered as well as used on another person. The technique can be performed by any layman, once he has been properly trained.

"My goal is to teach the method to anyone who might be a victim and everyone who might be a rescuer," said Dr. Heimlich. "The production and distribution of this film goes far toward achieving that goal."

Within the year since the method was first published in a medical magazine, it has been credited with saving more than 225 lives and has received much publicity. Dr. Heimlich has also made several public appearances demonstrating the technique.

"It is important that the Heimlich Maneuver is properly administered and I realized that a film which demonstrates the technique could reach hundreds of thousands far more quickly and effectively," Dr. Heimlich said. "That's why I became involved in the production of this film and I am encouraging the use of this vital film wherever and whenever emergency lifesaving procedures are taught."

"How to Save a Choking Victim: The Heimlich Maneuver" may be ordered by writing to: J. Michael Hession, Paramount-Oxford Films, 10105 Logan Drive, Potomac, Maryland 20854. The cost is $225 a print.

FACT SHEET

"How to Save a Choking Victim: The Heimlich Maneuver"

11 Minutes   Available in: 16 mm
                                      Super 8 Cartridge
                                      Videotape

                    Spanish Language Version

Price:	$225—Sale
	$ 30—Rental
	Please make checks or purchase orders payable to: Oxford Films.
Subject:	Film identifies three clues indicative of a person choking to death. It demonstrates the simple four-step method for saving lives developed by Dr. Henry Heimlich, director of surgery, Jewish Hospital, Cincinnati, who also appears in the film.
Suitable Uses:	Training film in health and safety education, emergency medicine, industrial medicine, first-aid courses, development of public awareness of choking as a major cause of accidental death.
Suitable Viewing:	Appropriate for all age groups.

G. Picket

You are working for the statehouse bureau of a press association and you receive a call from the press aide to Alexander Spivak, the Democratic candidate for the United States Senate:

> We just got back from Freeport where Al talked to a noon meeting of the Lions. The speech was the usual, but we have a situation there that can kill us with organized labor in the state and before you get a call from Bert Gentle of the union I want to give you our side.
>
> The Hotel and Restaurant Employees union pulled their people off the job at 9 a.m. We never knew it until we got there.
>
> Al didn't want to go in, see. But the club was waiting for him inside the Belmont Motel. There was a line in front, so we went in the back. You see, we didn't go through the line. Al wants labor to know he's for them, down the line. Here's a statement from him:
>
>> It is clear that labor has the right to a wage commensurate with the needs of men and women for a decent standard of living. In the legislature as a state senator I supported every wage and hour act introduced. I shall continue my support of the working people.

You call Gentle, who is director of the state office of the AFL-CIO, to see whether there has been any reaction. A secretary tells you Gentle will call back in 15 minutes. He does:

> Here's our statement on Spivak: "The local in Freeport informed the state office of the action of Mr. Spivak in the strongest language. They described his back-door entrance as subterfuge, and they ask the state office to reconsider its endorsement of his candidacy. We have scheduled a meeting for Friday at 8 p.m. in Freeport to discuss the matter with the local there."

In answer to your question about whether there is a possibility of action, Gentle says that in the past he knows of only one occasion when an endorsement was revoked. There have been, however, occasional censures. You read him Spivak's statement and ask for a reaction.

Gentle says, "Officially, nothing. Off the record, that's the usual baloney."

Write 200–250 words.

10 Making Words Work

Skill Drill I: Spelling

The 50 words below are some of the most frequently misspelled. Circle the correct spelling. Put a check mark next to the words whose spelling you would usually check with a dictionary.

_____ 1. (a) municipal	(b) municiple	_____ 26. (a) belief	(b) beleif
_____ 2. (a) cemetery	(b) cemetary	_____ 27. (a) privilege	(b) priviledge
_____ 3. (a) indispensable	(b) indispensible	_____ 28. (a) predjudice	(b) prejudice
_____ 4. (a) occurrence	(b) occurence	_____ 29. (a) their	(b) thier
_____ 5. (a) villain	(b) villian	_____ 30. (a) grammer	(b) grammar
_____ 6. (a) exhillirate	(b) exhilarate	_____ 31. (a) accommodate	(b) accomodate
_____ 7. (a) irresistible	(b) irresistable	_____ 32. (a) barberous	(b) barbarous
_____ 8. (a) consensus	(b) concensus	_____ 33. (a) athelete	(b) athlete
_____ 9. (a) committment	(b) commitment	_____ 34. (a) preceed	(b) precede
_____ 10. (a) nuclear	(b) nuculear	_____ 35. (a) arguement	(b) argument
_____ 11. (a) pronunciation	(b) pronounciation	_____ 36. (a) harrass	(b) harass
_____ 12. (a) existance	(b) existence	_____ 37. (a) repetition	(b) repitition
_____ 13. (a) illiterate	(b) iliterate	_____ 38. (a) definately	(b) definitely
_____ 14. (a) liaison	(b) liason	_____ 39. (a) disasterous	(b) disastrous
_____ 15. (a) nineth	(b) ninth	_____ 40. (a) exagerate	(b) exaggerate
_____ 16. (a) dissention	(b) dissension	_____ 41. (a) achievement	(b) acheivement
_____ 17. (a) developement	(b) development	_____ 42. (a) vaccum	(b) vacuum
_____ 18. (a) desireable	(b) desirable	_____ 43. (a) apparent	(b) apparant
_____ 19. (a) occasion	(b) occassion	_____ 44. (a) conscience	(b) concience
_____ 20. (a) nickle	(b) nickel	_____ 45. (a) dependant	(b) dependent
_____ 21. (a) alot	(b) a lot	_____ 46. (a) forty	(b) fourty
_____ 22. (a) referring	(b) refering	_____ 47. (a) embarrass	(b) embarass
_____ 23. (a) seperate	(b) separate	_____ 48. (a) interpetation	(b) interpretation
_____ 24. (a) similar	(b) similir	_____ 49. (a) assistant	(b) assisstant
_____ 25. (a) receive	(b) recieve	_____ 50. (a) allotted	(b) alotted

Skill Drills II: Grammar, Punctuation and Style

Each of these sentences has a writing error of some kind. Rewrite each sentence to eliminate the error in grammar, punctuation, style or usage.

Grammar

A. Leaping on his back, the horse galloped into the circus ring to applause.
B. The cook found he had insufficient condiments, he immediately stalked out of the kitchen.
C. Oil is it's leading export.
D. All departments lost business last year. Except furnishings and hardware.
E. He shot at the fleeing man. Hoping to hit him in the leg.
F. He said he was feeling alright but was still a little dizzy from the trip.
G. He looked up at the planes. Hoping to see the biplane he had been told was performing.
H. The plane went into a spin. Which thrilled everyone.
I. Its too late to help, he said.
J. Everyone hoped they could help.

K. The team played as though they wanted to win.
L. Before typing his story, the notes were arranged.

Punctuation

A. The two men each of whom had a hat pulled over his eyes entered the store.
B. To confuse them the owner busied himself at the rear.
C. He asked "What do you want?"
D. "Nothing." the taller one answered.
E. The childrens', mens', and womens' department lost money last year.
F. He took James' books and ran.
G. He asked who's book it is.
H. "Why do you want to know," he asked?
I. The question—which was shot out like a bullet, left him dazed.
J. He enjoyed daydreaming but some people thought him a little "loony."

Style, Word Usage

A. The major principal in writing is to make sense.
B. To weak writers, the proper words are often illusive.
C. Nevertheless, even weak writers like to be complemented on their work.
D. One of the marks of a weak writer is a lose style.
E. She ordered a box of monogrammed stationary.
F. Although there is a horde of some 400,000 words in English, weak writers have a vocabulary of fewer than 5,000.
G. Simple words from native tongue domineer good writing.
H. Milton's percentage of Anglo-Saxon words was 81, with 90 for Shakespeare, and the King James Bible runs around 94 per cent.
I. This doesn't mean a writer has to consultate the dictionary.
J. Just avert fine writing, jargon and colloquialisms.
K. This is excellent advise that effects us all.
L. The media is often blamed for establishing writing criteria that is copied without thinking by the public.
M. Less errors in newspapers would be helpful.
N. However, no one should imply all newspapers print poor writing.
O. Scarcely never do you see outrageously bad writing like you do in freshman compositions.
P. The true facts are sometimes difficult to face.
Q. Too much writing is discursively digressive and is wordy and verbose.
R. As a freshman, I for one, could always anticipate my instructor to literally cover my compositions with indecipherable red marks.
S. At that point in time, I thought I could write.
T. At this point, I know I can't.
U. He has his facts wrong.
V. Five bandits convinced a Brink's armored guard to open his truck door.
W A cement block building was destroyed.
X. Three persons died in the mishap.
Y. Its no fun trying to write but not knowing how.

Skill Drill III: Abused and Misused Words

Samuel Johnson, the 18th-century lexicographer and author, was riding in a closed carriage with several other passengers on a hot, dusty and long trip. As the afternoon wore on, one of the passengers, an estimable middle-aged woman, was obviously disturbed by the odor arising from the corner where Johnson was sitting. In those days, bathing was infrequent, and Johnson's personal hygiene was minimal. Finally, unable to hold back, the woman turned to Johnson: "Sir, you smell," she said.

"No madam," Johnson said, "You smell, I stink."

Found in a closet with the maid of the house, Mr. Johnson was upbraided by his wife: "Mr. Johnson, I am surprised." "No, madam." he replied. "You are astonished. I am surprised."

No reporter has to make these fine distinctions, although the precise use of language is one of the tools of the good news writer. Here are word couples often misused. Use them properly in sentences:

A.   affect-effect.
B.   allusion-illusion.
C.   angry-mad.
D.   bring-take.
E.   complement-compliment.
F.   council-counsel.
G.   emigrate-immigrate.
H.   flaunt-flout.
I.   farther-further.
J.   fewer-less.
K.   imply-infer.
L.   lay-lie.
M.   lend-loan.
N.   principal-principle.
O.   rebute-refute.

Exercise

A. Syracuse

Here is a handout from a sports publicity office. List all the clichés and trite expressions. Rewrite.

Syracuse, N.Y.—Syracuse University has 10 sophomore newcomers who may play more than a little football, but four of the young men could climb well up the ladder of success by December.

The athletes in question are halfback Ernie Davis, end Ken Ericson, center Bob Stem and quarterback Dave Sarette. The authority is Orange head coach Floyd (Ben) Schwartzwalder.

Top man among the rookie group is Ernie Davis, the fleet 6-2, 205-pound speedster from Elmira, N.Y., who was a world-beater with the SU frosh last fall and an All-American in high school. As the expression goes, Davis has all the tools.

"Ernie is our top prospect, no question about that," offers Schwartzwalder. "He'll be in our starting line-up against Kansas this Saturday and he's going to become a great football player. I'd like to have about 10 more like Ernie."

Ericson, a 6-2, 190-pound end from Weymouth, Mass., became an even more important factor in Schwartzwalder's plans last week when knee injuries sidelined starting left end Dave Baker and slowed up reserve flanker Tom Gilburg.

Ericson got a chance to scrimmage with the Syracuse starting team, due to the mishaps, and was very impressive. He is regarded as an outstanding pass receiver.

Stem, a fire-plug 5-11, 195-pound pivot from Phillipsburg, N.J., has improved by leaps and bounds and is pressing veterans Dave Applehof and Al Bemiller at center. Bob has drawn raves for his linebacking.

11 Fine Tuning the Story

Discussion

A. Readable

Clip from a newspaper stories that utilize these principles of good writing:

> Show, don't tell.
> Quotes that reflect the thrust of the event high in the story.
> Personification of the event through human interest illustrations or anecdotes high in the story.

Exercises

A. Artful

You are on rewrite for a New York City newspaper, and the court reporter in Brooklyn calls in with the following:

> Here's a little story that might be worth something. Fellow by the name of Arthur Howard, 28, of 585 Throop Avenue, was arrested for purse snatching. Magistrate Harry Serper is in charge of the court. When his case was called he told Serper he wanted a court-appointed lawyer. So Serper told him to sit down and wait.
>
> But when Serper called the case, Howard was gone. I asked around and one of the guards remembers a tall, thin guy who was moving slowly through the doors. Howard was tall and thin, so I guess it was the same guy.
>
> The piece is worth about 100–125 words.

B. Coach

WANTED RIGHT AWAY—a baseball coach
for 14 eight- to-eleven-years-olds who want to
compete in the Little League. Ask for Joe Pretz,
569–9884, or leave a message.

You work in Denver, Colo. Your editor shows you this classified advertisement from the *Clear Creek Courant* and suggests you call Joe Pretz and try to develop a story. You do. Mrs. Pretz calls Joe to the phone. He is 10 years old, and he tells you: "We can't play in the Little League when the games start June 14 unless we have a coach. There are 14 of us, 8 to 11 years old. We are all ready. Except for a coach. We have been practicing anyway. Everyone we ask is busy. No one has the time."

You ask Joe Pretz: "What's the best reason someone should coach your team." He answers: "Because we need a coach."

He tells you a friend, Bill Geiger, offered to help by placing the advertisement, and you call Geiger, who tells you:

"The boys are in the same pickle as Charlie Brown, you know. But there's no girls or beagles on the team."

You have a team roster, and you notice there is a name, Stacy Bartels, which could be that of a girl. You check. Stacy is indeed a girl.

Write a story with a Georgetown, Colo. dateline.

12 Broadcast Writing

Exercises

Rewrite for radio the following stories taken from the AP news wires. Keep the copy to between 50 and 60 words.

A. Solitary

SAGINAW, Mich. (AP)—Unruly students will again be placed in solitary confinement, in a decision by the Carrollton School District that is being protested by some parents and a school board member.

Under the program, names of students who misbehave are written on a chalkboard. After the fourth incident, students may be confined to one of three rooms—one 9 feet by 12 feet and two others 6 feet by 9 feet—for a six-and-a-half-hour school day, with two rest-room breaks and with lunch brought in.

David Pawley, a high school principal, said 21 of the school's 486 students had gone into solitary confinement since the policy went into effect at the beginning of the school year. The infractions covered by the policy include talking out of turn, walking around the classroom without permission and forgetting books for class.

The policy was scrapped last month after several parents complained. But the school board, in a 6-to-1 vote Monday, decided to reinstate it.

B. Hoofer

NEW YORK (AP)—A horse and a taxicab tried to negotiate the same Manhattan corner at the same time early today and the horse lost.

The horse pulling a hansom cab was about to turn left from Seventh Avenue onto 52nd Street when the taxi, making the same turn, cut the horse off, leaving the high stepper's right front hoof struck fast in the taxi's rear bumper, police said.

A fire rescue unit came and extricated the horse, who stood patiently by, according to John Driscoll of the rescue company. "He was a good horse," said Driscoll, who didn't get the horse's name.

Police didn't have it either, or the name of the cab and hansom drivers. It was just one of those unusual street occurrences, they said.

The horse did sustain a bad cut just above his hoof, but not bad enough to warrant a horse ambulance, Driscoll said.

The rescue team bandaged him up "just like a human" and sent him on his way.

"He just drove—or I should say rode—off into the sunset," Driscoll said.
AP-NY-05-10 05:16 EDT

C. Lakes

ORLANDO, Fla. (AP)—The 82 lakes that give Orlando its picture-card look will die without the infusion of millions of dollars and stringent drainage and pollution-control ordinances, a consulting group says.

The lakes, which get their water from rainfall and runoff, are victims of pollution washed from the city's growing expanse of roofs, driveways, parking lots and streets, according to a report released this week by the firm of Dyer, Riddle, Mills & Precourt.

Every lake in Orlando "has been degraded by stormwater and other pollutants to the extent that favorable conditions exist for excessive aquatic weed growth, large-scale algae blooms, possible fish kills and loss of recreational use," the report said.

D. Nukerock

NEW YORK (AP)—As they did with civil rights, Bangladesh and Vietnam, musicians are again getting involved. This time, it's nuclear energy.

A non-profit organization called Musicians United for Safe Energy (MUSE) announced Wednesday that they would stage two benefit concerts here next September with proceeds aiding anti-nuclear efforts.

David Fenton, a co-director, said the proceeds, estimated at "at least $1 million," from ticket and album sales will go to groups working for "a non-nuclear future and for safe energy technologies."

The proceeds will also be used to fund "an educational media campaign to bring the facts about nuclear power to the public," Fenton added.

Among those slated to perform at the concerts at Madison Square Garden on Sept. 19 and Sept. 20 are Jackson Browne, the Doobie Brothers, John Hall, Graham Nash, Bonnie Raitt and James Taylor.

Concert tickets will cost $18.50 and $15.50 and the performers are donating their services, Fenton said.

"The musical community reflects the renewed political interest in general," said one of the performers, Jackson Browne, at a news conference announcing the concerts. "I think people realize their lives are on the line."
AP-NY-05-10 04:03 EDT

Part 4 **Story Types**

---

13 Spot News Interviews and Profiles

EXERCISES

A. Flies

Roger Alexander, a biochemist who is chairman of the Friends of Nature, a national conservation organization, is in town to organize a state chapter. You are sent to interview him. He is 38, a graduate of Syracuse University, where he took his bachelor's and master's degrees, and Indiana University, where he received his Ph.D. He is married, father of two children, boy, 6, girl, 9. He is easygoing, smiles often, lives in Minneapolis, pays his own way to do organization work. He says:

Actually, I try to combine my vacation and any other work with organizing. I think conservation is perhaps our greatest domestic priority.

Not that it isn't of worldwide concern. Everywhere, people seem intent on pillaging nature. The story of Japan's industrialization is well-known. Air so polluted, babies must be given oxygen several times a day, water loaded with mercury. . . .

Instead of seeking the mastery of nature with unnatural means, we should learn to live with it in harmony and thereby derive pleasure from our niche on this planet. I mean by this that there are natural ways man can coexist. Take control of insects. We drop insecticides on our planet, poisoning the earth and ourselves in the process. But insects have natural enemies.

An entomologist, Philip B. Morgan, of Gainesville, Fla., has shown that the use of a parasitic wasp can control flies on the farm. He releases hundreds of thousands of these wasps—the technical name is Spalangia endius—near the fly breeding grounds. The female wasp lays her eggs in fly pupae. They grow and eventually kill their host.

In a month, the entire local fly population is destroyed. The wasps generally do not bother large animals or humans.

This is just one example of how we can use our great creative gifts to keep this perishable globe from disaster. . . .

We have a membership of 16,000 nationally, which is small. But we are not a mass organization. Our people are the doers. They influence legislation, give speeches. Of course, we are happy to have anyone. But we're not trying to overwhelm Congress with numbers but with the quality of our presentation. . . . Look, it's clear enough, isn't it? Dump sewage in the ocean, chemicals into rivers; dig holes in the deserts; pave over farmland; send deadly fumes into the air—we'll have destroyed ourselves by the end of the century. We can see disaster on the horizon.

B. Suspension

In an interview, Herbert Gilkeyson, the city schools superintendent, tells you that because of a Supreme Court decision that grants students facing disciplinary action the right to a hearing, he has adopted a new code for disciplinary hearings. Write a story of 300–350 words. Here are your notes:

1. We will notify all students that if they are called for a disciplinary hearing, they can defend themselves by having an attorney present.
2. There will also be an appeal process set up at the school.
3. The Supreme Court states the student can appeal beyond the school to the court system.
4. The new policy will take effect at the beginning of next semester. We need a little time to set up the situation here.
5. Included in this new policy will be a clear statement of what can lead to a student's suspension—use of alcohol or drugs on school grounds; profane or obscene language; destruction of school property; disturbance in class; fighting; injuring others; disrespectfulness.
6. The penalty for a violation is ten days suspension. Repetitions may lead to expulsion.

In answer to your question of whether the new policy is more stringent or lenient than the present one, Gilkeyson replies:

In a way, it is tougher. We have been permissive in the past, and some teachers have not known what the grounds for suspension are. They tended to let things go, profanity, for example. Now they know it is clearly an act that can lead to suspension if they decide the behavior is out of hand.

You ask about the number of suspensions last year. He says:

Last year, we had 178 in the high school system and 53 in the intermediate grades. I'd say that's about average for a city of this size.

I have no idea what will happen under the new policy. Obviously, a teacher will know his or her charges must stand up under questioning from an attorney, so petty violations will be ignored.

You ask for his opinion of the Supreme Court ruling:

I think it's sound. Of course, it is something of an intrusion into the school system. But since the Supreme Court's decision in *Tinker v. Des Moines,* it has been clear that the Court believes students have constitutional rights. And they should.

Our only desire is to run a good school system where children can learn in a safe, helpful and constructive environment. The troublemakers will be out, even with the new Court ruling.

C. Galloway

You have been sent to interview a foreign correspondent, Joseph L. Galloway Jr., who will be speaking tomorrow night to journalism students at the local college. You have been given his background and have quotes from your interview. Galloway is well-built, of medium height, has close-cropped hair. Write 400 words.

Background
Joseph L. Galloway Jr. was appointed Moscow bureau manager of United Press International in 1976. Galloway has been a UPI correspondent for 15 years, the last 12 in a variety of assignments in Asia. Before going to Moscow he was manager for Southeast Asia with headquarters in Singapore. He also has served in New Delhi, Jakarta and Tokyo. Before going to Asia, he worked for UPI in Kansas City and Topeka, Kansas.

He was a combat correspondent in Vietnam and was nominated for the Pulitzer Prize for his war coverage in 1965. He was among the final American correspondents in Saigon before it fell to the North Vietnamese in 1975.

He was born Nov. 13, 1941 in Bryan, Texas, and attended Victoria College in his native state. His quotes:

Given the time and material, a person who has learned the basics of brick-laying can build a grand cathedral. Without those basics his structures will turn out to be hollow and dangerous shells.

It is no different for the reporter.

A good police-beat reporter can cover the White House, and perhaps more of them should.

The basics for the reporter from station house to White House are accuracy and fairness— honest information honestly conveyed.

The reporter owes a lifelong debt to his editor, his readers and, above all, to himself. The ledger on that debt is updated and balanced every time he touches a typewriter or a VDT or a microphone.

He owes all parties the debt of full, fair, balanced coverage of a story which he should approach with personal interest, personal knowledge and a personal commitment to the truth.

There are no routine stories, only stories that have been covered routinely.

Beginning reporters are traditionally "broken in" with a tour of writing obituaries, considered a small, ho-hum, backrow operation of no seeming consequence.

What nonsense. What an opportunity.

The obits are probably read by more people with greater attention to detail than any other section of a newspaper. Nowhere else is error or omission more likely to be noticed.

A good reporter gives each obit careful, accurate handling and searches in the stack for the one or two that can be brought to life.

"Veteran of WWII," the funeral-home sheet says. Did he make the D-Day landing on the beaches of Normandy? "Taught junior high English for 43 years." Find some former pupils who can still quote entire pages of Longfellow because somehow she made it live and sing for them.

Look around. See who's likely to go before long and interview him. Few people can resist the opportunity to tell of their life and times. The good reporter finds them, listens to them, and learns from them.

Whatever the assignment, look for the people, listen to their stories, study them—and in your copy let them move, speak, act naturally. Put no high-flown words in mouths that never spoke them. You write of real people, not puppets to be yanked around from paragraph to paragraph, and you owe them their reality.

Check your facts. The more startling the claim, statement or allegation, the more attention should be given to double or triple checking for error or misinterpretation.

A good reporter is a student all his life. Each new assignment demands a crash course in the theory and practice of yet another profession or system. From station house to courthouse to state house or White House, you have to find out what the official sitting in the chair knows, and you cannot recognize the truth from a position of blind ignorance.

Reporting involves long hours of listening to those who do know the ins and outs of the story, digging in the morgue files, filling up another shelf in the bookcase at home.

Then there is always the continuing study of your job as a reporter and writer whose challenging subject is the changing and unchanging conditions of mankind. For that study, you must read.

The prescription "to read" by itself does not convey what I mean.

If in this electronic era you are not accustomed to it, then you must train yourself to gulp down the printed word with the true thirst of someone who has covered the last 15 miles of Death Valley on his belly.

Read for your life.

Read every newspaper that comes under your eye for style, for content, for ideas, for pleasure. And the books, my God, the books. The world of modern publishing has a 500-year headstart on you and it is pulling further ahead every year.

Never mind your transcript or your resumé. Let me see your bookshelves at home and your library card.

In a long career, a reporter's assignments may change radically and often, or he may spend his lifetime on a single beat in one town. That is a matter of personal choice, opportunity and chance. What never changes is the basic debt owed and the only way to settle it.

I served my apprenticeship on a small Texas daily, sitting at the left hand of a fine, conscientious reporter who handled the city government beat. He had been there for years then and today—20 years later—he is still there. In amazement, I heard him turn down job offers from big city dailies. He knew and encouraged my own ambitions, but his ambition was simply to continue providing honest, informative coverage of his beat.

His explanation:

"You may go and cover the great capitals of the world and the great conflicts, and that's an important job. But unless the people of this town, and all the other towns like it, know and understand the workings of their own city hall, how can you expect them to understand what is happening 6,000 miles away? Unless there's someone doing my job right, your job is hopeless."

D. Criticism

You are told that Frederick Cole, a retired editor of newspapers in Florida, California and Michigan, is in the city to serve as an adviser to your newspaper, which plans to revamp its makeup and coverage. Your editor tells you that Cole has strong feelings about journalism education and he tells you to interview Cole for a 350–450 word piece.

The editor says Cole is 68, never went to college, was a successful city hall, legislative and White House reporter by the time he was 30 and then became city editor of *The Chicago Sun.* He went on to *The Houston Chronicle, The San Francisco Examiner,* and he was executive editor of a group of newspapers in the Chicago area, the Atlas Newspapers, since absorbed by other newspapers in the area. He retired about a year ago.

Your editor tells you that it would be a good idea to find out as much as you can about journalism education before seeing Cole, and you first make a list of material you want to dig up in references: the number of students now enrolled in journalism schools, in past years; the number of accredited schools; recent articles about journalism education.

You next make up a list of questions for Cole. You have heard that he thinks journalism students are not well prepared for their jobs. You list questions along those lines.

You then interview Cole at his hotel. He is white-haired, has a ruddy complexion, is thin, of medium height, wearing a dark blue suit. He has a strong grip when you shake hands and he often smiles, as if to reassure you that he is not really the ogre he is made out to be.

Here are some of the quotes you note for your story:

I still think of myself as an editor, and I talk that way. Can't get the business out of my system. I was a copy boy when I was 16 and I never graduated from high school. But in my day, eighth grade was terminal. A high school boy studied Latin, algebra and read the plays of Shakespeare.

Anyway, the newsroom was an education. We had sports reporters who knew the archaeology of Greece, and city editors who could recite French poetry. Not many. But enough to tell a kid that there was more to this business then fires and murders. I learned it all.

I'm not sure that youngsters take to learning the way we did, and this is showing up in the young men and women who come into the newsroom as beginners. Editors and educators have a common objective: We want to strive for optimum quality in our newspapers. And, to do that we need each other.

What we need to do is candidly appraise the weaknesses of today's journalism education—and then do something about it.

Too many applicants lack a working knowledge of the English language. Some can't even type. Others can't spell.

Half of the aspirants who come into my office think a board of supervisors is plural. And they see nothing wrong with a sentence such as "The Chamber of Commerce will hold their annual meeting tomorrow night."

Many of them are hunt-and-peckers on the typewriter, and most of them can't type 30 words a minute. Their spelling is atrocious. I've found that fewer than half of them can't spell such commonly used words as 'accommodate,' 'commitment' and 'judgment.'

They are still being taught that a good lead includes the Five W's and an H. There's little evidence they ever were taught that a reader's degree of understanding drops off dramatically for each word over 20 in a sentence.

We're getting too many hopefuls who lack a background in economics, literature, philosophy, sociology and the natural sciences. They know little of local government. And they can't even report to the office on time.

Do the applicants we're getting have imaginative minds? They think they do because, when using words of attribution, they come up with every word they can think of but the one that usually is the best to use: "said."

That's not the kind of creative thinking we're looking for. We want young reporters who have enough imagination to go after the stories that are not usually done and to write them with a style and flair that will excite our readers.

And none of them can cope with the pressure of deadlines. When they must write fast, they tie up.

Sure, we expect a lot because we don't label our stories—written by a beginner, intermediate or advanced reporter. Our readers pay for a professionally done product.

How important is spelling to today's editors? We wouldn't even consider hiring a reporter who can't pass our spelling test. If he can't spell, we don't care how many prizes he won in college.

My advice to journalism educators is:

—You should be turning out graduates who want jobs in the 'general practice' of newspapering rather than specialization. That will come later.
—If your students can't write or can't spell, counsel them—or flunk them out. You'll be doing them a favor, for we don't want them.

Maybe it's time to be more demanding about applicants for the journalism major. I'd make all students who want to study journalism take spelling, punctuation and grammar tests as well as force them to write an essay from a set of facts so that we can see whether they can an use the right word in the right place.

I think there may be too many students in journalism right now. Many are going to be terribly disappointed because they simply are in the wrong field. Journalism requires an outlook, a mental discipline, a curiosity and, above all, a willingness to work hard day and night.

Skill Drill: Necessities

Every story may be said to demand certain necessary information. It is the reporter's task to include the information in the story. List the information that would be required in the following stories:

A.   **Fatal:** A traffic accident in which a person died.
B.   **Lieutenant:** Promotion of a local serviceman.
C.   **Project:** Announcement of a new construction project.
D.   **Blaze:** A fire that destroys a building in town.
E.   **New:** Appointment of a new teacher, clergyman, city official.
F.   **Game:** The result of a football or basketball game.
G.   **Verdict:** The verdict in a trial.
H.   **Death:** The obituary of a former city official.
I.   **Clinic:** Proposed closing of a neighborhood public health clinic.
J.   **Zone:** Request for a change in zoning classification from residential to commercial.
K.   **Queen:** The election of a campus beauty queen.
L.   **Crime:** The annual city-wide crime report.
M.   **Split:** A divorce filing.
N.   **Damage:** Suit alleging $250,000 damages for injuries in an auto accident.
O.   **Meters:** Introduction of an ordinance to get rid of parking meters downtown.

14 Capturing the Spoken Word

Exercises

A. Council

Write a story based on the following notes from a local city council meeting last night. Use all the facts here. The council decided:

1.   To build a viaduct across railroad tracks at Johnson Street, scene of three automobile-train accidents in the last seven months. To cost $300,000.
2.   To dismiss George Q. Banks, welfare director. Successor not appointed. Banks criticized last month for "irregularities in finances of department" that the city manager found in audit.
3.   To add new inspector in department of sanitation. Appointed David Lowe. He has been assistant bacteriologist at Fairlawn Hospital.
4.   To hold referendum at next election (May). Citizens to vote on $1,000,000 bond issue for replacement of sewers throughout downtown area. Present system in use since 1884. Leakage into ground water supply; system inadequate for load.

   Sewer construction is the first part of 10-year city-core regeneration plan. Traffic rerouting next; then downtown mall.

B. Reject

An organization known as the Concerned Parents Association two weeks ago presented a petition to the local school board asking for the removal of several books from the public schools. The association, which includes members of the three major religious groups and various racial and ethnic groups, has in past years confined its activities to submitting material, much of it used, to encourage brotherhood studies in the schools. The books it asks to be removed are, according to the list of the group: "Manchild in the Promised Land," by Claude Brown; "Laughing Boy," by Oliver LaFarge; "The Fixer," by Bernard Malamud; "The Adventures of Huckleberry Finn," by Mark Twain; "Portnoy's Complaint," by Philip Roth; and "Down These Mean Streets," by Piri Thomas.

Five of the seven members of the city school board today issued the following statement at a news conference. The five are Albert Swimmer, Helen Epstein, Charles Thorne, Jean Silver and Salvatore Vincent. Thorne, the president of the board, reads this statement:

We intend to vote against the request when the board discusses the petition by the Concerned Parents Association next Monday. We have been holding meetings with teachers, parents and students, individually, as we promised two weeks ago when the matter was presented to the board.

Several members of the association have been speaking to us, and although we believe we have heard ample evidence for the association's point of view, we certainly do not intend to prohibit them from speaking at Monday's meeting. It is possible that new arguments will be presented at that time.

However, we have heard the supporters, read the books, spoken to many of those involved. The argument of the association and its supporters is best summed up by the statement of Mrs. M. Richard Farrington, who asks, "Why do they have to tell it the way it is? Some of these books print downright filth. As for Jim, in Huck Finn, he is portrayed as simple, superstitious, childlike, no role model for young blacks."

We agree that some of these books are realistic. Claude Brown's book does use street language, and it goes into detail about heroin use. Huck Finn is a subversive book; it does subvert the values of a society Twain disliked.

We respect the intention of these concerned citizens. But some arguments are as silly as the parent in a California school who asked that "The Red Badge of Courage" be removed from schools because she thought it was about a Russian war decoration.

We are also concerned that should we act as we are requested we would violate the law as stated by the U.S. Supreme Court. The appeals court said that a school board violates First Amendment guarantees if it removes books already on the library shelves. The court said:

Here, we are concerned with the right of students to receive information which their teachers desire them to have. . . .

A library is like a storehouse of knowledge. When created for a public school, it is an important privilege created by the state for the benefit of the students in the school. That privilege is not subject to being withdrawn by succeeding school boards whose members might desire to winnow the library for books the content of which occasioned their displeasure or disapproval.

In answer to a question, Swimmer, who is black, says:

These books do denigrate certain groups. But that is only their superficial message. Each of them is written with a passionate regard for the dignity of mankind.

But what happens when books are censored? Well, the immediate reaction here is that the popularity of these books has increased, school officials tell us. But for precisely the wrong reasons. In the long run, censorship is disastrous, for once censorship begins, it will not stop.

Epstein is asked if the charge that "The Fixer" has anti-Semitic stereotypes has some validity. She answers:

I leafed through the book the other day after a few years, and I can see how someone would object, just as I would understand reactions to "The Merchant of Venice" and "Oliver Twist."

Clearly, Shylock and Fagin are anti-Semitic stereotypes. There is some debate about Shylock, who at times is a sympathetic character. But there is none about Fagin. Yet, what good is served by censoring the books? Perhaps it is true that youngsters who cannot understand that these books reflect certain periods and feelings should not be asked to read them.

I'd agree that small children have no business reading "Manchild," but I read "Huckleberry Finn" to my 12-year-old daughter and she thought Jim was a wonderful human being.

She is asked about "Portnoy's Complaint": Would you want your daughter to read it?

Well, I wouldn't want her to have Portnoy for a boy friend when she grows up. At her age—she's 12—she should not be exposed to that kind of book. But I see nothing wrong with having it on the shelves of the high school library and using it in the class for seniors.

Write a column of copy.

C. Astrology

Albert Sherman, professor of physics at the local college, Mallory, is a speaker at the luncheon of the annual meeting of the college science club. As the newspaper's science reporter you decide to attend because the topic sounds intriguing: "Astrology is Bunk."

Here are some of your notes. Write a 250–300 word story.

Astrology has millions of followers in this country. Generally, no harm is done by it. Reading the daily charts in the newspapers is as harmless as following Dick Tracy or Peanuts.

But some people do take astrology seriously. They make business decisions, marry, and mate on the principles of the solar stirrings as interpreted by the astrologer. . . .

Astrologers defend their field vigorously, but it is really quasi-scientific occultism. They talk about scientific research, but they pay only lip service to the search for scientific validation of evidence. . . .

What distinguishes science from pseudo-science is its method. Some of these principles are:

Falsibility—if the hypothesis is not true, you will get a negative result.

Replicability—different researchers will derive the same results.

Intersubjective verifiability—agreement between the advocate and his critic on the standards for verifying claims.

Astrology does not subject itself to these tests.

Finally, one of the simplest tests we use in science is a logical principle known as Occam's Razor. This says that when given two equally satisfactory explanations of an event, you take the simplest.

Incidentally, students ought to think of that when they do their own research. Nature is not complex. It loves order and simplicity.

But in the case of the astrologers, their work is a complex of signs, conjunctions and couplings whose interpretations no one agrees on.

Divining the fate and future of human beings from the positions of the stars and other heavenly bodies is ancient man's way of understanding the universe, not modern man's way.

D. Driving

You are assigned to cover a talk at the luncheon of the Freeport Rotary Club, at the Barton Hotel. The speaker is Johnson J. Burdette, vice president in charge of statistical analysis for the Travelers Home Assurance Co., of Chicago. His subject: "How to Cope with the Mounting Traffic Toll." Your deadline is an hour after the speech concludes. Here is the prepared text:

Thank you, Bob. It's good to be in Freeport, this wonderful town my grandparents traveled through on the way west. It's changed a lot since then, and haven't all of us? And not for the better, I suppose. In those days the pace of life was set to the speed of the human being. Now we've got to adjust to the speed of the machine. I wonder if we'll ever be able to do it. The human body and mind are fragile things indeed. I wonder if we were designed to cope with all we're subjected to. I know that even what we call a leisurely speed on the highway is enough to break every bone in a man's body if there's an accident.

This is what I want to talk to you about today . . . death on the highway, not a pleasant subject, but a pressing one when you consider that more people have been killed on our highways—many more—than have been slain by the enemy in all our wars.

Highway fatalities are our number one cause of accidental death. Every year, some 50,000 men, women and children die in grinding traffic accidents.

We're not making much progress in cutting this toll, although some years we drop a bit, particularly in 1974 during the fuel crisis, when the speed limits were set at 55 miles per hour and the high gas prices led to less driving. There were 46,400 fatalities then. But in 1977, we passed 52,000, and in 1980 we exceeded 53,000.

In California, they were killing each other at the rate of 10 a day. And not even the biggest, widest, best-lighted highways seem to stop the carnage. Death knows no holiday on the highways.

"Separate traffic lanes" was the cry we heard some years ago. So we built freeways on which it is possible to drive for miles without seeing a car coming in your direction. Yet the motorists insisted on wrapping their cars around trees, running off the road and in general doing to themselves what we thought they would not do.

What, then, is the answer? But first, let me ask: Do we want an answer? For there is no one who can say that he has not been touched by a traffic death—of a relative or a good friend. Personally, one of my best friends died just a month ago when his car ran off the road late at night.

John left a widow and three children, and how they are going to manage I don't know. I suppose Sue will have to go to work. And I imagine Ted and Betsy will have to drop out of college, at least until they can earn enough money to pay for another year.

These are the human dimensions behind the cold statistics you see in the newspapers.

I ask you again, what is the answer?

There is no single solution. In fact, it is absurd to talk of trying to eliminate all traffic deaths. It cannot be done. There are certain factors we cannot control.

But there are some that we can. We know, for example, that seat belts cut down on fatalities in collisions. They should be used by every driver and automobile passenger. I'd like to suggest a few lesser-known areas where action is possible. First, let me tell you what I do **not** have in mind.

I don't believe in billboards exhorting drivers to slow down. If they are soberly presented, the driver never sees them. If they are garish enough to attract his attention, he sticks his neck out of the window to read and the next thing he knows he's broken his neck on the turn he never saw.

I don't believe in slogans . . . slow down and live . . . don't mix drinking with driving . . . don't drive if you are tired.

The fact is that most deaths occur at normal driving speeds, in daylight when road conditions are fine. And whoever heard of stopping a drinking driver by asking him to turn down that last cocktail?

No, I propose what I think are realistic methods. First, a tightening of driver's licensing tests and next a toughening of law enforcement.

In many states, the drivers license examination is a farce. It is far from strict—takes only a few minutes, and the agency doing the testing usually suffers from fiscal malnutrition. Testers are insufficient in number to give detailed examinations. Eye testing equipment is not used or is so old as to be worthless. So the incompetent driver, the physically handicapped driver, gets a license. My point is:

Don't let him get behind the wheel in the first place. Driving is not a right—it's a privilege, one which the state can give and can take away. I say: Make the giving tougher.

And make the taking away easier.

We find that in about one fourth of fatal accidents, one or both drivers had been drinking. This is a phenomenal figure. It does mean that drinking and driving don't mix. But you won't stop it by asking the drinker not to drive. We must have laws that define drunk driving at .10 alcohol content of the blood, not .15. Then take the license away on the first offense. Not permanently, but for 30 to 60 days. Long enough for the drinking driver to be genuinely concerned. On the second offense, no license for a year. And the third . . . permanent revocation and jail.

And this can be done only by law officers who are really interested in doing the job . . . who are supported by the local organizations—clubs such as yours—and the newspaper and leading citizens.

Too often a patrolman simply takes the keys away from a drinking driver and puts him in a taxi. That way the patrolman is signing someone's death warrant. And it might be your child's.

The patrolman doesn't want to handle the driver this way. But he feels he has to. The community wants him to. Oh, he will arrest the fellow driving an old Chevy or a battered Ford. But in the small town or the medium-sized city he will take the well-dressed drunk home. Or maybe the prosecutor will charge him with reckless driving instead of drunk driving in order to obtain a quick conviction.

Now these are only two steps. Yet I am certain . . . as certain as statistical analyses can lead me to be . . . that they will cut our traffic deaths in half.

Your editor tells you to write almost a column.

E. Cecil

You are covering a talk given by John R. Hunt, the Cobalt bureau manager for the *North Bay* (Canada) *Nugget*. Hunt has been with the newspaper since 1952 and writes a widely read column. Presume that the talk was given to one of the local service clubs at a luncheon. Write 250–300 words.

My car was making a funny noise the other day, so I took it to one of those antiseptic palaces, where I described the symptoms to a nice young lady, who called in a distinguished-looking gentleman with a stethoscope around his neck and a certificate on the wall which announced that he was a doctor of motors.

My car was taken away while I sat in a luxurious waiting room, reading old magazines and wondering what the experts were doing. Eventually I was told that my car was ready. I was presented with the bill and wrote a check, then drove frantically to my bank, where I persuaded the manager to cover it, and by the time I got home the car was making the same funny noise again. So I went for a beer at the Legion, and bumped into Cecil, the retired mechanic.

Cecil is retired, most reluctantly, because he is just about 65 years old. He doesn't see too well, because he always insisted on using a cold chisel without any goggles and got a chunk of steel in one eye, and then he damaged the other eye because he insisted on using a welding torch, again, without any goggles.

But oh, how I wish Cecil, and all the other old mechanics I have known, were still in business today.

They didn't wear white coats; in fact, they were usually in grease from head to foot. They didn't use a stethoscope. Cecil could stick his thumb against the block, feel the vibrations and tell you if you needed new spark plugs, new points, or a ring job.

Cecil was a man of very strong opinions and ran his own garage for years. In fact, he refused to work on my car for a long time because he was a dog lover, and when I was a member of the local council, I hired a dog catcher who picked up Cecil's dog. Cecil beat the dog catcher to a pulp and paid a heavy fine. But he also refused to work on my car, or any one else's car who supported dog catchers. In fact, I believe he refused to work on the town truck, with the result that our snow-removal program was paralyzed.

If you called Cecil out late at night, he took a pair of pliers and some baling wire and a hammer. If he couldn't get the car to start with minor adjustments, he would attack it with the hammer and beat it into submission.

If you visited Cecil in his garage, you didn't sit in a waiting room. If you were lucky, you found an old crate or an orange box, and generally you took some newspapers with you to spread or you would have to take your clothes to the cleaners. And, if Cecil liked you, he would direct you to the back of the shop, where you could usually find some potent antifreeze and a fairly clean tin cup.

But Cecil could take the motor out of a Chevy and put it into a Ford, welding new mounts and making new connections. He could take some beat-up jalopy that a teenager had paid twenty bucks for, and make it sing like a bird. And, if Cecil told you that your car was finished, you didn't argue, you had it towed to the dump.

And, when you got a bill from Cecil, you shoved it in your hip pocket and told him that you'd settle up on pay day, or maybe later, and he would only chuckle, or let rip with a few cuss words, and then crawl back into his grease pit and flail away with his hammer.

There are still a few Cecils out there. Running one-man garages, charging moderate bills and doing a good job. If you know one, cherish him, treat him gently, even buy him a drink, because as cars grow more complicated, and motorists more helpless, the Cecils of the automotive world are a precious and rare breed. But, I'd take him, covered in grease smelling of booze and swearing like a trooper, in preference to all the white-coated doctors of motors that I know.

F. Nixon

Assume this is Nov. 7, 1962, and you are a correspondent for a large morning newspaper that has assigned you to cover the gubernatorial race between Edmund G. Brown and Richard M. Nixon. The race is of national interest because Nixon had run for the presidency in 1960 and had been narrowly defeated by John F. Kennedy. Nixon, it is thought, can use the California governor's office to keep in the eye of the public. Brown is the incumbent, but Nixon is given a good chance to win since he carried the state in the 1960 election, 3,259,000 to 3,224,000.

At 10 a.m., when the gap between Brown and Nixon has widened to some 250,000 votes, Nixon sends Brown a telegram of congratulations. Herbert Klein, Nixon's public relations man, leaves the Nixon suite in a Beverly Hills hotel where you and other newsmen are gathered in the lobby. Klein says that Nixon will not attend the news conference. Instead, Klein will hold the conference. After 10 minutes, a Nixon aide enters the lobby and says Nixon will appear immediately. He enters.

At 49, Nixon has waged a vigorous campaign. This morning he is drawn and tired looking. Although he smiles now and then as he speaks, he seems angry. He speaks without a script, and as you listen you realize what he is saying is so important that you will have to obtain a transcript as quickly as possible. Since you have two hours to deadline you are able to wait for the transcript that is being made from a tape cut by ABC radio network and *The New York Times*. Here is the transcript. Write at least 900 words.

Good morning, gentlemen. Now that Mr. (Herbert G.) Klein (Nixon's press secretary) has made his statement, and now that all members of the press are so delighted that I have lost, I'd like to make a statement of my own.

I appreciate the press coverage in this campaign. I think each of you covered it the way you saw it. You had to write it the way according to your belief on how it would go. I don't believe publishers should tell reporters to write one way or another. I want them all to be free. I don't believe the F.C.C. (Federal Communications Commission) or anybody else should silence (word lost in transmission).

I have no complaints about the press coverage. I think each of you was writing it as you believed it.

I congratulate Governor Brown, as Herb Klein has already indicated, for his victory. He has, I think, the greatest honor and the greatest responsibility of any governor in the United States.

And if he has this honor and this responsibility, I think that he will now have certainly a position of tremendous interest for America and as well as for the people of California.

I wish him well. I wish him well not only from the personal standpoint, because there were never on my part any personal considerations.

I believe Governor Brown has a heart, even though he believes I do not.

I believe he is a good American, even though he feels I am not.

And therefore, I wish him well because he is the governor of the first state. He won and I want this state to be led for courage. I want it to be led decisively and I want it to be led, certainly, with the assurance that the man who lost the campaign never during the course of the campaign raised a personal consideration against his opponent—never allowed any words indicating that his opponent was motivated by lack of heart or lack of patriotism to pass his lips.

I am proud of the fact that I defended my opponent's patriotism.

You gentlemen didn't report it, but I am proud that I did that. I am proud also that I defended the fact that he was a man of good motive, a man that I disagreed with very strongly, but a man of good motives.

I want that—for once, gentlemen—I would appreciate if you would write what I say, in that respect. I think it's very important that you write it—in the lead—in the lead.

Now, I don't mean by that, incidentally, all of you. There's one reporter here who has religiously, when he was covering me—and incidentally, this is no reflection on the others, because some of you, you know, weren't bothered. One reporter, Carl Greenberg—he's the only reporter on *The* (Los Angeles) *Times* that fits this thing, who wrote every word that I said. He wrote it fairly, objectively.

I don't mean that others didn't have a right to do it differently. But Carl, despite whatever feelings he had, felt that he had an obligation to report the facts as he saw them.

I am saying these things about the press because I understood that that was one of the things you were particularly interested in. There'll be no questions at this point on that score. I'll be glad to answer other questions.

Now, above everything else I want to express my appreciation to our volunteer workers.

It was a magnificent group. Five hundred thousand dollars was spent, according to *Newsweek* magazine, to get out the vote on Election Day. They had a right to do that if they could get the money. We didn't have that kind of money. But, believe me, we had wonderful spirit.

And our 100,000 volunteer workers I was proud of. I think they did a magnificent job. I only wish they could have gotten out a few more votes in the key precincts, but because they didn't, Mr. Brown has won and I have lost the election.

I'd like to say a word nationally. I know that some of you are interested in that. I have not been able to appraise the results for the Congress because not enough of them are in.

I only understand that we approximately broke even. Is that correct—in the Congress?

Well, at least that's what I have. Do you have a report on the Congress—any of you? It's about even?

Q.—The Democrats picked up some.

A.—They picked up some?

Q.—Some in the Senate and

A.—Oh, I know in the Senate they did. Yeah, Bob, I understood that, but in the House, I understand we picked up five in the House. We can't tell, because California isn't in on that yet.

Well, the most significant result of this election was what happened in four major states: Rockefeller's victory in New York, Scranton's victory in Pennsylvania, Rhodes' victory in Ohio, Romney's victory in Michigan—means that in 1964 the Republican party will be revitalized.

Now, it will be revitalized, of course, provided the Republicans in California also can under new leadership—not mine—because I fought the fight and now it's up to others to take this responsibility of leadership, and I don't say this with any bitterness, because I just feel that that's the way it should be.

But the Republican party under new leadership in California needs a new birth of spirit, a new birth of unity, because we must carry California in '64, if we are to carry the nation.

But when you look at New York and Pennsylvania, Ohio and Michigan and the solid Republican Midwest, 1964 is a horse race.

I say this was no indication that I don't think that President Kennedy has immense popularity at the moment—popularity which came out as a result of his handling of the Cuban situation.

But, on the other hand, now the problems arise: What will happen in Cuba? Can we allow this cancer of Communism to stay there? Is there a deal with regard to NATO? Is there going to be with regard to NATO and the Warsaw pact? Are we going to continue any kind of an agreement in Cuba, which means that Khrushchev got what we said we would never agree to before he made his threat with regard to his missiles and that is, in effect, ringing down an Iron Curtain around Cuba?

These are the things that Mr. Kennedy, of course, will have to face up to, and I just hope—and I'm confident that if he has his own way he will face up to them if he can only get those who opposed atomic tests, who want him to admit Red China to the U.N., all of the wooly heads around him—if he can just keep them away from him and stand strong and firm with that good Irish fight of his, America will be in good shape in foreign policy.

Domestically—I'm answering these questions because I know that some of you will ask them—domestically, the economy needs to get going again. The Cuban thing, of course, has had a tendency to obscure that. A lot of defense contracts have come into California and other areas. I'm not complaining about it. That's the way the political game is played.

But I do feel that it is important that the economy get going again and I trust that through tax reform or some other device, relying on individual enterprise and individual opportunity, that the economy will get going again.

To me, more important than anything else, America has got to move now. It's got to move forward economically, with productivity. It's got to move forward—I'll say it in the presence of my good friend from Britain here—Ed Tetlow (of *The London Telegraph*)—its got to move forward relying on individual enterprise and individual opportunity.

One last thing: What are my plans? Well, my plans are to go home. I'm going to get acquainted with my family again. And my plans, incidentally, are, from a political standpoint, of course, to take a holiday. It will be a long holiday. I don't say this with any sadness, I couldn't feel, frankly, more—well, frankly, proud of my staff for the campaign they helped me to put on. We campaigned against great odds. We fought a good fight. We didn't win. And I take the responsibility for any mistakes. As far as they're concerned, they're magnificent people, and I hope whoever next runs in California will look at my staff and take some of these people—use them—because they are—they're great political properties, shall we say, putting it in the—in a very materialistic way.

One last thing: People say, What about the past? What about losing in '60 and losing in '64? I remember somebody on my last television program said, "Mr. Nixon, isn't it a comedown, having run for President, and almost made it, to run for Governor?" And the answer is I'm proud to have run for Governor. Now, I would have liked to have won. But, not having won, the main thing was that I battled—battled for the things I believed in.

I did not win. I have no hard feelings against anybody, against anybody, against my opponent, and least of all the people of California. We got our message through as well as we could. The Cuban thing did not enable us to get it through in the two critical weeks that we wanted to, but nevertheless we got it through and it is the people's choice.

They have chosen Mr. Brown. They have chosen his leadership, and I can only hope that that leadership will now become more decisive, that it will move California ahead and, so that America can move ahead—economically, morally and spiritually—so that we can have character and self-reliance in this country. This is what we need. This is what we need to move forward.

One last thing. At the outset, I said a couple of things with regard to the press that I noticed some of you looked a little irritated about. And my philosophy with regard to the press has really never gotten through. And I want to get it through.

This cannot be said for any other American political figure today, I guess. Never in my 16 years of campaigning have I complained to a publisher, to an editor, about the coverage of a reporter. I believe a reporter has got a right to write it as he feels it. I believe if a reporter believes that one man ought to win rather than the other, whether it's on television or radio or the like, he ought to say so. I will say to the reporter sometimes that I think well, look, I wish you'd give my opponent the same going over that you give me.

And as I leave the press, all I can say is this: For 16 years, ever since the Hiss case, you've had a lot of fun—a lot of fun—that you've had an opportunity to attack me and I think I've given as good as I've taken. It was carried right up to the last day.

I made a talk on television, a talk in which I made a flub—one of the few that I make, not because I'm so good on television but because I've done it a long time. I made a flub in which I said I was running for Governor of the United States. *The Los Angeles Times* dutifully reported that.

Mr. Brown the last day made a flub—a flub, incidentally, to the great credit of television that was reported—I don't say this bitterly—in which he said, "I hope everybody wins. You vote the straight Democratic ticket, including Senator Kuchel." I was glad to hear him say it, because I was for Kuchel all the way. *The Los Angeles Times* did not report it.

I think that it's time that our great newspapers have at least the same objectivity, the same fullness of coverage, that television has. And I can only say thank God for television and radio for keeping the newspapers a little more honest.

Now, some newspapers don't fall in the category to which I have spoken, but I can only say that the great metropolitan newspapers in this field, they have a right to take every position they want on the editorial page, but on the news page they also have a right to have reporters cover men who have strong feelings whether they're for or against a candidate. But the responsibility also is to put a few Greenbergs on, on the candidate they happen to be against, whether they're against him on the editorial page or just philosophically deep down, a fellow who at least will report what the man says.

That's all anybody can ask. But apart from that I just want to say this:

Among the great papers in this country that the people say that I should be concerned about— *The Louisville Courier Journal, The New York Post, The Milwaukee Journal, The Fresno* and *The Sacramento Bee*—I couldn't be—disagree with that more. I want newspapers—if they're against a candidate I want them to say it. I believe they should say it. I don't mind reporters saying it. I would hope that in the future, as a result of this campaign, that perhaps they would try at least simply to see that what both candidates say is reported, that if they have questions to ask of one candidate they ask the same questions of the other candidate.

The last part. I leave you gentlemen now and you will now write it. You will interpret it. That's your right. But as I leave you I want you to know—just think how much you're going to be missing.

You won't have Nixon to kick around any more, because, gentlemen, this is my last press conference and it will be one in which I have welcomed the opportunity to test wits with you. I have always respected you. I have sometimes disagreed with you.

But, unlike some people, I've never canceled a subscription to a paper and also I never will.

I believe in reading what my opponents say and I hope that what I have said today will at least make television, radio, the press first recognize the great responsibility they have to report all the news and second, recognize that they have a right and a responsibility, if they're against a candidate, give him the shaft, but also recognize if they give him the shaft put one lonely reporter on the campaign who will report what the candidate says now and then.

Thank you, gentlemen, and good day.

15   From the Office and on the Beat

Exercises I: Accidents

A. Pedestrian

From the police reports: James Reynolds, 48, sign painter, 35 West Borden Ave. Struck by automobile at Johnson and Elm Streets, 4 p.m., Fairlawn Hospital. Critical injuries, including skull fracture. Car driven by Robert F. Magione, 872 Ogden. Says pedestrian stepped into intersection suddenly. No charges. Investigation by Officer Sigmund Gerter.

A call to the hospital indicates that Reynolds is in intensive care. Write for morning newspaper.

B. Three Dead

State highway patrol responds to your check with the following information: Collision on Route 16 where it intersects with State Highway 40, 18 miles north of town. Three dead, all in the car coming out of Route 16: Stanley Shaeffer, 68, of 45 Marvell Ave.; his wife, Mildred, 65, and granddaughter, Anne Shaeffer, 17, of Chicago, who was visiting her grandparents while en route to Boston University where she was to be a freshman student. The second car was driven by Louis Kruger, of Hutchinson, Kansas. Kruger was taken to Fullerton Hospital for treatment of leg fractures and internal injuries. Time: 11 p.m.

Investigating officers, Albert Doris and Ben Sandler, said the Shaeffer car was turning into 40 and had apparently not stopped for the stop sign. Possibility Shaeffer had a stroke. Write for afternoon newspaper.

C. Truck

Call from stringer in Clovia, nearby suburb, with a fatal: Irwin Soto, 22, of Clovia, was killed instantly at noon on access road four miles west of town. Police say he apparently had a flat and had stopped to fix it, propping his pickup truck up with a bumper jack. Somehow he got under truck, it slipped, and he was crushed. Severe chest injuries, said the doctor, Frank Rand, on Soto's arrival in Clovia hospital.

He is survived by parents, Jack and Eileen Soto, of Clovia; his widow, Alice; and an infant daughter, Adeilada. Funeral services pending. Body at Clovia Funeral Home. He was a local boy who played in all the high school sports and was a star sprinter. He spent two years at the University of Tennessee on a track scholarship but came home to run his father's dairy farm two years ago.

Exercise II: Fires

A. Suspicious

It is 8:30 p.m. and you hear on the police radio that a fire has been reported at Crosson Cafe, 127 Dakota St., a downtown location. You arrive with a photographer and see a lot of black smoke but not much fire.

The chief of the fire department, Damon Maguire, says that the fire originated about 20 minutes ago in the basement where extensive damage was done. It did not spread upstairs into the dining area, he says. No one was injured.

But 20 diners were forced to leave by the smoke. A few are still milling about, and you speak to two, Scott Ryan of 1580 East Millerton Ave. and Kelly Serpa of 46 Barton St. "We were having steaks when suddenly the smoke started coming up through the floor and around the walls," Ryan says. "A couple of women started to scream," Serpa says, "but all I was worried about was that my New York cut was going to be well done, and I like it rare."

You call the owner, Ralph Crosson, two hours later. He says he has insurance to cover the loss he estimates at $15,000. He says a diner reported seeing two young men running from the scene, and you check with fire and police officials and they verify that the fire seems to have been purposely set. They suspect arson.

You ask Crosson if he has any idea who might have started it. He says he recently fired a dishwasher who said he "would get even."

"You might check with the police and see if they have located the fellow. Name is Chip Ramsgate, and I think he lives on Olive Avenue."

You check back with the police, but the officer in charge will not release any further information.

Write for a morning newspaper.

Exercises III: Police and Crime

A. Drugs

Your editor hands you this story and tells you that he wants a more dramatic lead, even if you have to neglect the today angle. Rewrite the story.

A Biddeford youth is scheduled to be arraigned in district court here today on charges of possession of a narcotic and resisting arrest.

Police said that the youth, Mark Reib, 18, was arrested yesterday after a downtown foot-race between Reib and two sheriff's officers.

Police said Reib tried to obtain narcotics from the Stuben Drug Store on Main Street by giving false information over the phone.

The caller claimed to be a Biddeford physician and said the prescription would be picked up shortly. The store clerk became suspicious and notified local police, who were waiting for the pickup to be made.

The chase occurred after Reib left the drugstore, police said.

Reib was freed on $5,000 bail, pending arraignment.

B. Arrested

The police announce the arrest of Carl Morton on a charge of murder. He was sought for six days in the slaying of Mildred Miller, 47, a pianist who lived at an inexpensive hotel, The Plaza, 912 Washington Ave., where Morton also had a room. The police announced at the time of her slaying that she had been strangled and raped. The slayer had also set her bed afire and taken a television set and radio.

Det. Sgt. Richard Raskover said that Morton had been sought because Mrs. Miller's radio was found in his room. His girl friend, who was not identified by the police, said Morton had left the night of the slaying after depositing the radio in their room and telling her he had just sold a television set and was going out to buy some food.

When she asked Morton where he had obtained the radio and television set, Raskover said, he told her not to tell anyone about them.

Morton was picked up at a downtown hotel this morning. Police would not disclose how they learned of his whereabouts. But it is a well-known police procedure to question hotel clerks about new guests.

Raskover says that Morton will be questioned about several other deaths in The Plaza. Four women died there within the past six months under strange circumstances. All were past 60.

He did not resist arrest. No bail is set on capital charges.

You ask if Morton has a record and Raskover suggests you obtain that information elsewhere. Through a contact you learn Morton was born in 1945, was arrested in 1968 on a robbery charge and sentenced to 2½ to 5 years in the state penitentiary. Three years later he was sentenced to 90 days on a misdemeanor, loitering, after his arrest for possession of dangerous drugs, a felony. In 1973, he again benefitted from plea bargaining, being sentenced to 90 days for attempted theft following his arrest for robbery in the second degree and criminal possession of stolen property, both felonies.

Write a 300 word story.

C. Drowning

Here is a police report filed at the Long Beach Police Department of an accidental drowning. Presume that you are the police reporter and picked up the report at noon on the day of the accident.

Because of the various newsworthy elements in the story, your editor gives you as much space as you think the story requires.

POLICE DEPARTMENT
CITY OF LONG BEACH

DEAD BODY (ACCIDENTAL DROWNING) REPORT   Case No. _____

Classification of Crime   CORONER'S #70-2264

VICTIM'S NAME (Firm name if business)	RESIDENCE ADDRESS	RESIDENCE PHONE
FRAZIER, Nathaniel	FROM: US ARMY -USERPAC (KOREA)	

NAME OF BUSINESS WHERE VICTIM WORKS	BUSINESS ADDRESS	BUSINESS PHONE (Area Code-Ext.)
U.S. ARMY (enroute) to:	CONUS - Future Assignment: 426th Signal Corps. FORT BRAGG, N.Carolina	

WORKING HOURS–DAYS OFF	DATE COMMITTED: DAY OR WEEK	TIME COMMITTED
	Thrs. 2/26/70	Approx. 2:45AM

LOCATION OF OCCURRENCE	NAME OF PREMISES
4217 East Ocean Blvd., Motel Swimming Pool	Beach & Oceanaire Motel

PERSON REPORTING OFFENSE	RESIDENCE ADDRESS	(714)846 2154 PHONE	DATE AND TIME REPORT
GAMBRIL, Donald L.	16702 Bolero Lane, Huntington Harbour, Calif.		2/26/70 6:30AM

	INVESTIGATING OFFICERS (Last name, initials)	DIV. FILED BY
	NJ LUDWIG & NV ERIKSEN	W#1 PATROL

VICTIM'S: SEX, RACE, AGE, AND OCCUPATION (If Juv. D.O.B.)	PROPERTY ATTACKED (Type Bldg., Public Street, Vehicle, etc.)
M. Negro 22yrs. U.S. ARMY (DOB: 8-21-48)	Motel Swimming Pool

CRIMES AGAINST PROPERTY HOW ATTACKED (Point where entry made)	CRIMES AGAINST THE PERSON HOW ATTACKED (Method used)

MEANS OF ATTACK (Instrument–method used)	MEANS OF ATTACK (Weapon–force or means used)
DEAD BODY	

OBJECT OF ATTACK (Property taken or obtained)	OBJECT OF ATTACK (Apparent Motive–Type of property taken or obtained)
ACCIDENTAL DROWNING	

1. ADDITIONAL SUSP'S. 2. ADDITIONAL VICTIMS. 3. WITNESSES 4. DESCRIBE CRIME–VICTIMS/WITNESS STATEMENTS –NAME OF OFFICER/PERSON FINDING EVIDENCE–WHERE EVIDENCE FOUND–OFFICER'S INVESTIGATION. 5. ITEMIZED DESCRIPTION OF ANY PROPERTY TAKEN, INCLUDING SERIAL NUMBERS AND VALUE. 6. IF SUSPECT ARRESTED LIST NAME AND BOOKING NUMBER.

Officers on patrol 4200 block Ocean Blvd. Oceanside Parking lot were contacted by the R.P. GAMBRIL, who stated to officers that there was a negro boy at the bottom of the swimming pool of the Motel located across the street. Officers immediately went to the scene accompanied by the R.P. and observed the victim, a male negro, lying on the bottom of the deep end of the swimming pool. Officers further observed that rigor mortis had set in as victim's body only touched the bottom of the pool in the trunk area, and victim's arms and legs were partially outstretched in a rigid position. Officers also observed victim to be clad in plaid Bermuda shorts, red and black in color.

Officers notified the station via police radio of the situation, requested Fire Dept. and a Homicide Unit to Roll.

Officers then went to the office area and contacted the Motel owner: POLLMAN, Earnestine, who resides at this address. Officers in questioning the owner, found that she had no male negroes registered as guests in her motel. Officers at this time started checking vehicles in the area and contacting other guests in the motel in an attempt to learn the identity of the victim. During officers' investigation, a Fe. White from Room #22 came to the edge of the pool, observed the victim, she started to cry and ran quickly back to her Motel Room. CONTINUED

TECHNICIAN NOT REQUESTED	TECHNICIAN REQUESTED	X SPECIAL REQUEST		
MARKET VALUE OF PROPERTY	DICTATED BY NJ LUDWIG	DATE AND TIME DICTATED 9:25AM 2/26/70	ELECTRONIC SEC.	DISPATCH

ADDITIONAL INFORMATION TO BE ADDED TO REPORT MADE AND
FILED COVERING CASE MENTIONED ON FILING MARGIN

Victim: FRAZIER, Nathaniel   Date 2/26/70
         Coroner's #70-2264
Accused   No.

PAGE #2

DEAD BODY (Accidental Drowning) - continued

Officers at this time went to Room #22 and contacted the occupants who
identified themselves as Mr. KERN, Edward and his wife Nancy of 251 South
Clarkson, Denver, Colorado, Area #303 #722 7239. Mr. Kern stated to officers that he was in Long Beach on business for his employer, STEARNS-
ROGER CORPORATION. He further stated that the evening prior he went to
the Los Angeles International Airport to pick up his wife, who arrived at
the airport on the evening of Feb. 25th. While Mr. & Mrs. Kern were at
the International Airport they became acquainted with the victim who was
also accompanied with a Marine Sergeant, name unknown. They stated that
both men were flying-Military Standby, out of Los Angeles, and were waiting for a flight to their destination. Mr. Kern stated that it was their
first wedding anniversary, and that the two soldiers had asked them to
have a drink with them, and they all four went to the Tower Restaurant,
where they became better acquainted over a small bottle of Champagne. He
further stated that during the course of the evening the victim had consumed three more mixed drinks (Rum & Coke). As they were leaving the airport, the Marine Sergeant caught a flight out, but the victim learned that
the first available flight to his destination would be at Noon on
2/26/70. Victim stated to Mr. Kern that he would spend the night in the
Airport, but Mr. Kern insisted that he return to Long Beach with them, as
he had an extra bed in his motel room, and victim could sleep there, and
he would drive him back to the Airport in time to catch the flight next
day.

The victim and Mr. & Mrs. Kern returned to Long Beach, to their motel.
Victim and Mr. Kern went next door to THE TRAP BAR, where they both consumed one glass of beer and played some pool. They then returned to the
Motel Room at approximately 2:AM 2/26/70, at which time Mr. & Mrs. Kern
retired for the evening. Victim stated to them that he would go to bed in
a few minutes, but before he did, he wanted to dangle his feet in the
swimming pool for a while, and borrowed a pair of Mr. Kern's Bermuda
Shorts. Mr. & Mrs. Kern stated that when they went to bed the victim was
sitting by the edge of the pool in a lawn chair, smoking a cigar, and
they did not miss him until the time Mrs. Kern came out of the apartment
while officers were on the scene and observed him in the bottom of the
pool. The Kerns stated the victim had told them that he could not swim.

Officers at this time contacted R.P. Gambril who stated he was the Swimming Coach at Long Beach State College, and the reason for his presence
at the Motel this morning 2/26/70, is that there are numerous Russian
Swimmers staying at the Motel - with whom he is associated. He further
stated that the victim was initially found by MOORISEV, Alexei, who had
advised Mr. Gambril thru an interpreter, MALISHEVA, Maya (Fe.W. 43 yrs),
that he had gone to the pool area this morning to swim, at which time he
observed the victim, and immediately told MALISHEVA to contact Mr. Gambril.

                          CONTINUED   NJ LUDWIG 10:02AM 2/26/70

                          Report by
P.D. 151   Typed by: HE Petersen   same

ADDITIONAL INFORMATION TO BE ADDED TO REPORT MADE AND
FILED COVERING CASE MENTIONED ON FILING MARGIN

Victim: FRAZIER, Nathaniel   Date 2/26/70
           Coroner's #70-2264

Accused   No.

PAGE #3

DEAD BODY (ACCIDENTAL DROWNING) continued

Officers contacted Motel guests in adjoining rooms, but located no one who heard anything unusual, except for a Mrs. R.L. GOODENOW, 401 Stuart St., Wall Lake, Iowa, who is on vacation and staying in Room 20. Mrs. Goodenow is Fe.W. 62yrs. and stated to officers that at either a quarter till three, or a quarter till four, she heard some loud splashing, and went to the window and looked out. She stated she observed someone swimming in the pool, and occasionally she would see an arm splashing across the surface, but merely thought it was an underwater swimmer, as the tenants who checked into the Motel were advised by the owner, that there were numerous Russian Swimmers staying at the motel, and oftentimes would be swimming at unusual hours.

Coroner was advised and an investigator responded and arrived on the scene, at which time the body was removed from the bottom of the pool by the Fire Dept. and the body was placed at the edge of the pool where the Coroner made his preliminary examination. As the body was raised to the surface and exposed to the atmosphere, officers observed a large amount of thick mucous type material flowing from the victim's nostrils and mouth, which is known as lung purge, and common in drowning cases.

The mortuary of the Month - Dilday Mortuary - was called and they picked up the body. The body will be transferred to Hunter's Mortuary as this mortuary has a contract with the Military, and handles all Military personnel.

                                NORMAN J. LUDWIG & NORMAN V
                                ERIKSEN
               Report by   10:32AM 2/26/70
             Typed by:HE Petersen   same

P.D. 151

D. Cookies

Your editor likes short features—he calls them "brights"—from the police beat, and the following information from a crime report sounds like a good "bright":

> The day care center of the Central Berkshire Regional School District holds its classes in the basement of the United Methodist Church, 850 Johnson St. During the evening, a basement

window on the north side of the building was broken and the basement entered. Margaret Reeder, the director of the center, said all that appeared taken was a carton with four boxes of chocolate cookies. She says the cookies were so stale the children wouldn't eat them and the center was planning to return them.

E. Crime Reports

Total crimes, Precinct No. 18.

	Last Year	Previous Year
Total Crimes Reported	1,844	1,753
Auto Thefts	262	202
Theft from Motor Vehicles	556	468
Burglaries	673	610
Purse Snatching	55	55
Robbery	265	378
Murder	6	6
Rape and Attempted Rape	16	18
Possession Dangerous Drugs	11	16

The city police department released city-wide totals on crimes reported for last year which your newspaper ran yesterday. You go to Precinct No. 18, in which the local university is located, in order to write a piece on crime in that area since it was the subject of intensive police action after a record number of crimes, 3,299, were reported in the precinct three years ago. As you see, the year following the transfer of additional officers to the precinct, the number of crimes dropped to 1,753. Last year, the number inched upward.

Police Captain Stanley Solomon tells you that the situation in the precinct is "steady," that the figures "reflect a citywide trend over the past two years of higher property thefts in middle and upper income areas. We have always been a prime area for auto thefts. These foreign cars are attractive for some reason. Also, people around here tend to be absent minded, and there are always the newcomers who think they're back home where they never locked their car doors. Anyone with a stereo or a camera in full view inside a car is asking for trouble."

The precinct, No. 18, includes the northwestern part of the city. In the immediate area around the university, described as Police Post No. 3, total crimes reported went from 148 two years ago to 220 last year, the largest increase in the precinct. Most of the crimes involved thefts from motor vehicles (81) and burglaries (103). Write 300 words for the local newspaper. Then write the first four paragraphs of a story for the campus newspaper.

F. Bite

In making routine checks of major hospitals, you are told at 2 p.m. that a police officer has been admitted with a severe dog bite. The admitting clerk at Denver General Hospital identifies the officer as William Trevor, age 39, of 1250 Humboldt St., Denver. His condition is good. His injury is a dog bite to the right wrist. He was brought to the hospital by ambulance at 1:15 a.m. (today) after being picked up at that address. That is all the information she can give you.

Next you reach the public relations office at the hospital and ask for additional information. In response to questions, and after checking with others at the hospital, Beverly Collins, the director of public information, tells you that Officer Trevor has been treated with antibiotics to ward off infection from inch-deep bites to the bottom and top of his wrist. The bites reached the bone. He has been given a sedative and is resting quietly. He is expected to be released from the hospital tomorrow. He is not to take shots to prevent rabies, because the city's standard dog-bite form, which was completed by ambulance attendant K. L. Ross, indicates that the dog has been seized by an animal control officer and is being held for observation in the city dog pound. You are told that the officer is asleep and cannot be disturbed by a telephone call.

You go to the police records room, where you learn there is a written report of the incident. It was prepared by Patrolmen B. J. Kirby and A. M. Dunning. It is headed "Attempt Burglary." It says that at approximately 12:45 a.m. (today) at 1250 Humboldt St., an attempt was made to burglarize Apartment 205, the home of William Trevor. The body of the report reads as follows:

Victim states that he was in the bedroom when he heard the balcony door open. Door is sliding type and was unlocked. Victim got out of bed, turned on light situated on bedside table and obtained service revolver, .38 Police Special, from holster in chair. On entering living room victim spotted white male, age approx. 30, in room. Victim stated, 'Hold it right there,' and suspect turned and ran out of sliding door. Victim aimed revolver to fire, but as he was about to fire victim's dog became excited and bit victim. Victim taken to DGH with dog bites to right wrist.

The report describes the suspect as wearing a Mickey Mouse T-shirt and blue jeans but no shoes.

You check with the personnel department of the police department and are told there is no William Trevor on the Denver Police Department. You re-check the offense report and note that Trevor's business address is listed as "Sheridan P.D." You call the police department in Sheridan, a suburb of Denver, and reach the police chief, Irving Scillicide. He confirms that William Trevor is a member of the Sheridan police force. He is assigned to the K-9, or dog unit. You ask Scillicide if he knows what happened. He tells you, "It's my understanding Bill surprised a burglar in his apartment and struggled with him, and Rusty bit Bill instead of the burglar. It's a damn shame when a police dog bites the wrong person."

Write 150 words.

Exercises IV: Obituaries

A. Ibbotson

You are working on the staff of the *Hawk Eye* of Burlington, Iowa, and receive this form from the editor. He tells you he wants a basic obituary, nothing more than is contained below.

Name **Mrs Agnes Viola Ibbotson former Burlington** resident **7101 Twana Dr.**
Age Yrs. **85** Months Days Usual Residence **7101 Twana Dr.**
Place of Death; Hosp. or Residence **7101 Twana Dr.**
City **Urbandale** County **Polk** State **Iowa**
Time and Date of Death **8:02 PM Tuesday April 13, 1976** Length of Stay in Place of Death
Birthplace & Date **Sept. 5, 1890 Morning Sun, Iowa**
Fathers Name & Address (deceased) **Harry McDonald** Age
Birthplace
Mother's Maiden Name (deceased) **Elizabeth** Hines Age
Birthplace
Deceased Marital Status **Widow** Wife's Maiden Name
Date & Place of Marriage **Eugene Burton Ibbotson Oct. 1912 He died Nov. 1948**
Usual Occupation & Years Spent **Housewife** Yr. Retd.
Religious Affiliation **Grace United Methodist Church**
Organizations

Military Serv.; Name of War Place & Date of Enlistment
Place & Date of Discharge Ser. No.
Branch of Service Rank

Education

Survivors: Spouse	**Dec.**		Address	
Children;				
	Mrs Gladys Goss		Burlington	
	Mrs Vera Gibbs		West Burlington	
	Mrs Verlee Johnson		Burlington	
	Mrs Arlene Walker		Urbandale, Iowa	
	Donald		Mason City	
	Gene		Des Moines	

Parents	**Dec.**	Address
Brothers & Sisters		
John McDonald		Morning Sun, Iowa

No. of Grandchildren **16**   No. of Great Grandchildren **21**

Preceeded in Death by **Husband, 2 brothers and 2 sisters**

Services; Place **Lunning Chapel**   Time & Date **2:30 PM Friday**

Officiant **Rev. LeRoy Moore**   Denomination   Address

Interment **Kossuth Cemetery**   Sec.   Lot   Address

Time & Date   Place and time of other Rites

The Family will receive friends, or Friends may call at the **Chapel 7:30 until 9PM Thursday**

Remarks:

B. Perkins

You receive this paid advertisement from classified:

> **Perkins**—William F., of 1105 Madison Ave., on March 14, beloved husband of Josephine Parker Perkins. Service at Geo. T. Smith, Inc., 14 Laura Place, 10 a.m., Wednesday. Visiting hours 7 to 9 p.m., Tuesday. In lieu of flowers, contributions to Community Hospital Medical Center will be appreciated.

You telephone Mrs. Perkins and are given the following information:

Perkins was with O'Connor & Perkins, successor to Rich & O'Connor, which he joined in 1941. He was president of the state bar association in 1948 and had been active in the National Foundation for Infantile Paralysis, which no longer has that name because of the success of the Salk vaccine. He was chairman several years of the foundation's local chapter. He was born in Altoona, Pa.

He graduated from a college in Pennsylvania that is now Penn State, where he was a cross country runner. He went to Harvard where he was active in the Law Review and coached a soccer team made up of law students.

He died after a heart attack. He was 73.

Write four paragraphs.

C. Tsouprake

The following comes up from classified:

Tsouprake—Demetrios Athanasias, 560 Maple Street, on March 21, beloved husband of Juliana (Lappas); adored father of Natalie Arruzel, of Florence, Italy, and Christine Alice Costa, of New York City; grandfather of four; dear brother of Constantine, Stephen, George, Ann, and the late Chloe. Funeral service, Wednesday, March 26, 11 a.m., at the Greek Orthodox Cathedral of The Holy Trinity.

You obtain the following information. Write five paragraphs.

Age: 75.
Died last night in Community General, lung cancer.
Born: Greece.
Education: LL.D., Athens University.
          A.M., School of Political Science, Paris.
          LL.B., Stanford University.
Honors: Robert Kent Award of the Patent, Trademark and Copyright Research Institute of Oxford University, 1968.
          1958, U.S. delegate to the Lisbon Conference to revise the international treaty on patents.
Author: "Protection of Industrial Property."
          "Protection of Literary and Artistic Property."

D. Longo

An official of the B.C. Krebs Manufacturing Co. calls to tell you of the death from a heart attack in San Jose, Costa Rica, yesterday of Frank Longo, former personnel manager of the local company, which employs 250. He has prepared the following, which he dictates to you and which you should use as the basis for a story:

Longo was visiting his sister, Mrs. Rose Quintana, who lives in San Jose and is his only survivor. Longo was 78 and lived at 465 Lief Ave.

He went to work for the firm as a teenager after immigrating from Italy. Employed as a janitor, he worked up to inventory clerk within two years. As a clerk, he noticed the painstaking and cumbersome way in which inventory was kept and he devised an automatic system that was so successful it was copied by other large firms and eventually became the established procedure. Business textbooks referred to it as the Longo System, and it was in use until the introduction of the computerized inventory system.

Longo never had any formal education that we know of, but he was an omnivorous reader and donated books and funds to the local public library, which he called his high school, college and graduate school. He was made personnel manager at the age of 55 and completely changed the company's hiring system so that it became color-, sex- and age-blind two years later. He retired at 75.

He adds that the company telephoned Mrs. Quintana at noon to offer assistance. Longo will be buried there tomorrow. She said her brother had been a prudent investor and had an estate of $580,000. He left $250,000 to her and the rest to the local public library system.

Exercises V: Sports

A. Runner

Here are some notes from an interview with Arthur Baron, a biology major, who is a member of the Mallory College cross-country team that has just returned from finishing fourth at the NCAA Division III meet at Franklin Park in Boston. Baron finished eleventh—considered a good finish—and this is the second time he has been in the top 25 in the annual meet. The newspaper has had a story on the meet. You are to do an interview. Here are your notes.

Baron is 5'11", weighs 150, has brown hair, wears glasses.

Runs 20 miles a day—twice what most run—seven days a week in summer, lifts weights, and swims as part of his training. In winter, runs at least 10 miles a day unless snowbound. Yesterday, the day after returning from Boston, he did seven miles of road work in minus 20 degree temperature.

Baron says his coach, Steve Helmer, tries to develop internal motivation among the runners. "It's unlike high school where everything has a rigid schedule. Steve is more oriented to the athlete than the program. You're given credit for being able to think.

"At other schools, win-oriented coaches burn out their athletes. At some schools, the runners put in twice as much road work, but there is a point of diminishing returns.

"We have no athletic scholarships here, and there is no physical education major. None of us who ran in Boston came here to be athletes. We're here for the academic program. The coach knows that the Big Ten and other big conferences attract athletes. But running, the coach says, 'is for intrinsic reasons, not money.' "

Asked about the success of the team despite the small size of the school and its lack of scholarships, Baron says the team uses a tactic called "pack running." Instead of each running his race, the four stay together until the last mile. The effect on other teams is demoralizing, particularly when the four run in front, as they try to do.

"I could possibly run faster times away from the pack on my own, but there is a mental strain to running in front all alone. Also, the feeling of running with your team can cause you to beat a better runner."

Baron is thinking of studying medicine. The other three are going into science-related fields, physics, chemistry and biology.

A call to Helmer turns up the following information:

"Cross-country runners are highly disciplined and demand top performance of themselves. If there is a problem, it is that they do train to excess. They are very demanding.

"Cross-country runners in this country tend to come from the middle and upper classes and are good students, whereas the sprinters often are from less affluent homes. The situation in Egypt, where I spent a year, is reversed. There the military officers are the sprinters; the laboring class provides the long distance runners."

Write 400–450 words.

B. Trade

Willie Suarez, an outfielder with the local professional baseball team, the Red Sox, has been complaining about playing in the northern climate and has asked to be traded. He has played three seasons in Philadelphia and one season in windswept Candlestick Park in San Francisco. He is 28 and from Puerto Rico.

"Last season, my first season here, I felt the weather bad," he said in an interview last week. However, he batted .310 and drove in 101 runs. This year, after 50 games, almost one-third the season, he has 20 runs batted in and is hitting .274.

This afternoon you have a call from the Sox front office. The management decided to trade Suarez to the Braves in Atlanta. They received in return Dave Martin, a utility infielder batting .246 and a reserve outfielder, George White, batting .265.

You say you don't think the team received very much.

"Well, you might say we weren't getting very much from Willie either, and since he wouldn't play in cool areas, there wasn't much bidding for him. He's got great potential, but he'll kill his career with this kind of attitude."

Your ball club source says he can't be quoted by name but you can use the fact that it came from a person "close to the club."

The team is in fourth place, 12 games out of first.

Write 200–250 words, preferably with a delayed lead and a feature touch.

C. Reds-Braves

Here are the lineups and an inning-by-inning account of a baseball game between the Reds and the Braves. The Braves lead the Reds by two games for the division leadership before the game. Lemon is a left-hander, Katz a right-hander. Katz, 7-4, has lost two games to the Braves this year. Lemon, 11-3, has never faced the Reds. It is mid-season. There is no need to identify the teams any further or to place them in any league. (You could place them in the Western Division of the National League in a game between the Cincinnati Reds and the Atlanta Braves.)

First, devise the box score. Next, write a 400-word story for the morning newspaper. This is an evening game played in the Reds home town, your town.

Lineups

BRAVES	REDS
Bumiller, Ernie cf	Eddings, Bobby ss
Vorobil, Maury ss	Manoff, Stan lf
Weiner, Tommy rf	Douge, Harry 3b
Wallis, Mike lf	Cruz, Al 1b
Hand, Denny 3b	Marwell, Chuck c
Sherman, Gene 1b	Gougeon, Johnny cf
Day, Karl c	Kelso, Jack 2b
Weir, Rick 2b	Barrett, Eddie rf
Lemon, Carl p	Katz, Art p

Play by Play

First Inning
Braves: Bumiller walks on five pitches. Vorobil hits a 3-1 count to center-field wall; Gougeon makes putout. Weiner hits first pitch to center field for single. Wallis hits into double play, Eddings–Kelso–Cruz.

Reds: Eddings grounds out, Lemon to Sherman. Manoff looks at third strike. Douge flies out to Wallis.

Second Inning
Braves: Hand takes first when Kelso bobbles grounder. Sherman strikes out. Day singles to center, Hand going to third. Weir pops to Cruz. Lemon swings at and misses three pitches.

Reds: Cruz grounds out, Weir to Sherman. Marwell flies out to Weiner. Gougeon grounds out, Hand–Sherman.

Third Inning
Braves: Bumiller flies to Manoff. Vorobil singles to center. On one-one count to Weiner, Vorobil out trying to steal second. Weiner pops to Cruz.

Reds: Kelso fouls out to Day. Barrett hits 3-0 pitch to center-field wall for double. Katz grounds out, Sherman unassisted, Barrett taking third. Eddings flies to Weiner.

Fourth Inning

Braves: Wallis grounds to deep short and is safe on close play. Reds Manager Bordewich argues to no avail. Hand bunts Wallis to second, Douge throwing Hand out at first. Sherman grounds out, Kelso to Cruz. Wallis goes taking third. Day strikes out on four pitches.

    Reds: Manoff hits first pitch into left field stands for a home run, his 15th of the season, his 76th RBI. Douge grounds out, Vorobil to Sherman. Cruz pops to Hand. Marwell flies out to Wallis.

Fifth Inning

Braves: Weir singles on ground over second. Lemon sacrifice-bunts Weir to second, Cruz to Kelso, covering first. Bumiller tops pitch that dribbles toward third, and everyone is safe, Weir on third, Bumiller on first. Vorobil hits first pitch to deep center, Gougeon making catch. Throw to plate too late to catch Weir. Weiner grounds out, Eddings to Cruz.

    Reds: Gougeon hit on ankle by pitch, takes first. Kelso trying to bunt pops to pitcher who doubles Gougeon off first. Barrett flies to Weiner.

Sixth Inning

Braves: Wallis walks and steals second on 2-1 pitch to Hand, who then pops to Eddings. Sherman grounds out Kelso to Cruz. Day hits grounder past first, Barrett throwing Wallis out at plate on close call that Wallis protests vehemently and is warned by plate umpire.

    Reds: Katz grounds to Sherman unassisted. Eddings flies out to Hand in foul territory. Manoff grounds out Weir to Sherman.

Seventh Inning

Braves: Weir grounds out Eddings to Cruz. Lemon strikes out. Bumiller singles to left. Vorobil forces Bumiller, Eddings to Kelso.

    Reds: Douge walks on five pitches. Cruz singles to left, Douge going to second. Marwell hits into double play, Vorobil-Weir-Sherman, Douge taking third. Gougeon pops into center, Bumiller barely missing the catch, Douge scoring. Kelso forces Gougeon, Weir stepping on second unassisted.

Eighth Inning

Braves: Weiner flies to Barrett. Wallis doubles down first base line. Hand grounds out Douge to Cruz, Wallis remaining on second. Count goes to 3-0 on Sherman and Marwell goes out to talk to Katz. Calls trainer who examines Katz's hand. Blister is developing. But Katz says he is OK. (He has not pitched a complete game this year.) Sherman walks. Day grounds to third, Douge stepping on bag, forcing Wallis.

    Reds: Barrett flies out to Bumiller. Katz looks at three strikes, never lifting bat off shoulder, apparently unwilling to put stress on pitching finger with blister. Eddings flies out to Weiner.

Ninth Inning

Braves: Weir hits 3-2 pitch into center for a single. Ahearn pinch hits for Lemon; infield expects him to bunt. Ahearn swings at first pitch and it narrowly misses being fair past first. Infield drops back. Ahearn then bunts toward third and beats throw to first. Reds manager goes out for mound conference, leaves Katz in. Bumiller hits line drive to Kelso, who makes sideways leaping catch. Runners stay put. Vorobil hits into game-ending double play around the horn., Douge throwing to Kelso for the out at second and on to first.

    The game took two hours and four minutes, and the attendance was 16,069 paid.

D. Loser

You cover the local team, the Red Sox, and it has just lost 2-0 to the Phillies in an afternoon game. The winning pitcher was Randy Jones, the loser Bob Pierce. The Sox got six hits, the Phillies 10 off Pierce. The winning runs were scored in the fourth on a base on balls to Marty Balzer and successive doubles by Gene Mica and Tom Kemper.

You interview Ted Schmidt, the Sox leading hitter, after the game, who went nothing for four and struck out twice.

"I can't recall striking out twice in a game in my life in this league," he says. "But I did." He kicks his locker. "If I were a pitcher I'd be embarrassed to go to the mound with the kind of stuff Jones has. A nothing pitcher. Nothing."

You then talk to the Sox manager, Danny Appel, and you ask him about Jones. "A helluva pitcher. He's won 12 games and the season's one-third old. A lot of the guys say he's a nothing pitcher, but what you need to stay alive in this league is control and pinpoint pitching. The guys who have a lot of stuff but can't get it over the plate bomb out fast.

"Just between us, Schmidt had a bad day and was bitching. Christ, I'd give anyone on my team for Jones. The guy's worth a sure pennant to any contending team."

Jones is now 12-2 and Pierce is 6-5. The leading team in the league, the Pirates, lost a game in the standings to the Phillies by losing 5-3 to Montreal and the Phillies trail by two games.

Write a game story with a feature lead for a morning newspaper.

Skill Drills: Sports Vocabulary

Briefly, define, describe or identify the following:

Baseball

A. MVP

B. Pinch runner

C. Sacrifice fly

D. Save

E. Scratch hit

F. Texas Leaguer

Basketball

A. Dunk shot

B. Give and go

C. NIT

D. Top of the key

E.   Trailer

F.   Zone defense

Football

A.   Flanker

B.   Flare out

C.   Blitz

D.   Sack

E.   Tight end

Golf

A.   Eagle

B.   PGA

C.   Par four hole

D.   Slice

Hockey

A.   Face off

B.   High sticking

C.   Icing

D.   Red line

E.   Sudden death

Tennis

A.   Ace

B.   Double fault

C.   Mixed doubles

D.   Passing shot

Thoroughbred Horse Racing

A.   Claimer

B.   Fractions

C.   Maiden race

D.   Stretch runner

E.   Turf race

Exercises VI: Precedes

A. Planning

The secretary of the city planning board, Betty Forde, telephones to say that the regular board meeting scheduled for tomorrow night is called off because of the death this morning of the wife of the chairman, Philip Nicholson. The meeting, set for 8 o'clock in the city council chambers, will be held next Tuesday instead. Her name is Alice Nicholson.

B. Parade

The county volunteer fireman's association calls: It will hold its annual Kiddies Day Parade Sunday, May 7, beginning at 1 p.m. at Elm and Johnson and running down Elm through the city's business section to the grounds of the First Congregational Church where judges will make awards for funniest costume, prettiest costume, smallest pet and best float. On display at the church grounds will be the new pumper purchased last month. Last year, some 200 children from three to eight years took part. Mayor Sam Parnass will lead the parade, carrying his one-year-old daughter, Candy.

C. Recital

Telephone call from the parent association secretary and notes from the switchboard operator: Artur Rothstein, a French concert pianist, has donated his services for a recital in the music wing of the Horace Mann

School, Friday, 8 p.m. Tickets are $5. The concert will include Chopin's mazurkas and études, Beethoven's piano version of music from "The Magic Flute" and several works of Franz List. Proceeds will go toward the purchase of a high-fidelity system for the music department.

D. Appreciation

Here is a handout from the local chamber of commerce. It is marked for immediate release. Write two to three takes.

> Patterson Field will celebrate Patterson Field Appreciation Day, Sunday, beginning 1 p.m.
> The Junior Chamber of Commerce aviation committee will sponsor the program, which will salute the local field that is one of the nation's busiest airports not handling regular commercial or military flights.
> The field was opened in 1939. Since the field has been in operation there have been more than a million landings and takeoffs without a fatality.
> The program will open with an hour of plane rides for the public. Passengers will pay for the rides at the rate of one penny a pound for their weight. State officials are expected to attend.
> Demonstrations will include crop dusting and spraying and freefall parachute jumps. The Southwest Parachute Association will sponsor the jumps. The association president, Tom Slinkard, who has made 51 safe jumps, will lead three other association members in the 4,500 foot jumps.

You call the chamber public relations man, Thomas Everingham, to ask for the names of the state officials, and he tells you that William Sullivan, the state commissioner of aeronautics, and Lt. Gov. Harry Lee Waterfield will fly in, arriving about 1:50 p.m. to start the demonstrations. You ask for Slinkard's address. Everingham says that Slinkard lives at 2815 Yorkshire Blvd., but won't be there because he tripped off the back steps of his home and suffered a broken leg. But the demonstrations will be staged anyway. He says that the airplane rides will also be given from 3 to 6 p.m. At 4 p.m., the Sports Car Club will give an exhibition of skill driving at the southeast corner of the field. There will also be about 30 aircraft on display at the field in front of the Administration Building.

E. Poets

Student poets at Mallory College will hold a "Welcome Spring" poetry night in the Civic Auditorium April 3, 7:30 p.m. They will read their own and other works. Poet James Merrill will speak.

F. Lobby

(Call from Mildred Cahan.) The League of Women Voters will send a ten-person delegation to the state capitol, leaving 8 a.m., Monday, to talk to members of the state Legislature about a minimum wage bill, introduced last month and now in the Senate Labor Committee, that would exempt several types of workers from the state minimum wage law. To be exempted: hotel, restaurant and laundry workers, hospital aides, domestic workers, nonclassified municipal and state clerical workers. The local league last week endorsed the stand of the state organization opposing the bill. Mildred Cahan, chairman of the local chapter, said: "The bill clearly is aimed at the low-income female worker who now barely makes $3 an hour, a wage enabling her to bob up and down in a sea of poverty."

G. Trip

(Peter Hay, BPOE secretary, press release.) The local Elks Club announces that 42 of its members and their wives have signed up for a trip this summer to the Soviet Union and 16 will be going to China. The Russian contingent leaves July 15 for two weeks; the Chinese group leaves Aug. 15 for 15 days. One couple, Mr. and Mrs. Dale L. Himmelstein, 42 Ft. Washington Ave., will make both trips. "These will be our 21st and 22nd countries since Dale retired three years ago," Mrs. Himmelstein says. He was a clerk at United Airlines for 30 years "and never left the state until his retirement," she adds.

Exercises VII: Personals

A. Merit

Pamela Elman, 18, 1716 Palisades Ave., a senior in Dwight D. Eisenhower High School, won a National Merit Scholarship; $3,000. Will attend the University of Texas (Austin), as a pre-med student. The only one to win from this city; 3,500 in country. (Information from Bernard A. Meyers, principal.) Your newspaper's files have a story dated last year in which Meyers announces she is one of six students to have all A's in their first three years of high school work. In her freshman and sophomore years she was confined to a bed while undergoing treatment of spinal birth injury and took courses by special telephone. She has been in a wheelchair since then.

B. District Attorney

Paul Robinson, the district attorney, calls to say he will give a talk at a National Conference of Prosecutors convention in Chicago on July 23 where about 1,500 district attorneys will meet. His talk will be about the career-criminal tracking system that he says he has begun to use here. The system is designed to identify the frequent offender on arrest. An assistant district attorney is immediately assigned to the case and follows it, beginning with arraignment. "The purpose is to avoid plea bargaining with the resultant lenient sentences and probation for these offenders," he says.

Exercise VIII: Localizing

A. Appointees

On the following two pages is a release from the Federal Trade Commission. Rewrite for:

1. A newspaper in Boston.
2. A newspaper in Lexington, Ky.
3. The Associated Press wire.

FEDERAL TRADE COMMISSION news

WASHINGTON, D.C. 20580

FOR RELEASE 7am EDT, Friday September 5, 1975

FTC APPOINTS GERALD P. NORTON DEPUTY GENERAL COUNSEL
AND THOMAS LYNCH ADAMS, JR., ASSISTANT GENERAL COUNSEL

Federal Trade Commission Chairman Lewis A. Engman today announced the appointments of Gerald P. Norton, 35, to the newly created position of deputy general counsel, and of Thomas Lynch Adams, Jr., 33, as assistant general counsel for legislation and congressional liaison.

Norton's appointment is effective September 15, and Adams', August 4.

* * *

Norton has been assistant to the Solicitor General, Department of Justice, since 1973, and in that capacity has prepared and argued Supreme Court cases on behalf of the United States.

A native of West Roxbury, Mass., he received an A.B. degree (magna cum laude in economics) from Princeton University in 1961 and an LL. B (magna cum laude) from Columbia University Law School in 1964. At Columbia he was managing and research editor of the Law Review. Following graduation from law school, Norton was a law clerk to Judge Leonard P. Moore, U.S. Court of Appeals for the Second Circuit.

He joined the Washington, D.C., law firm of Covington & Burling as an associate in 1965, handling antitrust and other litigation until he joined the staff of the Solicitor General.

In creating the new position of Deputy General Counsel, General Counsel Robert J. Lewis explained that, "Because of Mr. Norton's extremely impressive credentials as a court room lawyer we expect to apply his experience principally to that area."

Norton is married to Amanda B. Pedersen, an attorney in private practice, and they live in Washington, D.C.

* * *

Adams had been legislative counsel for the Small Business Administration from early this year until his appointment to the FTC staff. From 1972 until early 1975 he was legislative assistant to U.S. Senator Marlow W. Cook and minority counsel for the U.S. Senate Commerce Committee. For two years prior to that time he was an attorney with the Land and Natural Resources Division of the Department of Justice. He was an officer in the U.S. Navy from 1963 to 1967.

A native of Lexington, Ky., he received a B.A. degree in history in 1963 from the University of Virginia. He was graduated from the Vanderbilt University Law School with a J.D. degree in 1970.

Adams is married to Anne Randolph, and they live in Washington, D.C.

# # #

PRESS CONTACT: Office of Public Information, (202) 963-4325
Arthur L. Amolsch, Director

REQUESTS FOR FTC DOCUMENTS SHOULD BE MADE TO LEGAL AND PUBLIC RECORDS, ROOM 130, FEDERAL TRADE COMMISSION, WASHINGTON, D.C. 20580. TELEPHONE (202) 962-5214).

1004–APPTGC

FEDERAL TRADE COMMISSION
WASHINGTON, D. C. 20580

OFFICIAL BUSINESS
PENALTY FOR PRIVATE USE $300

POSTAGE AND FEES PAID
U. S. FEDERAL TRADE COMMISSION

Exercise IX: Roundup

A. Pot

Your editor gives you a copy of the local college's current alumni bulletin and tells you to write a couple of pages on the article, "Marijuana—More Dangerous Than You Think." The author is Nicholas Trowbridge, the chairman of the college psychology department.

Many students believe that marijuana is harmless, and they contend that there is ample scientific evidence to support their contention. To put it another way, they say that there is no proof that it is harmful. College students, with their newfound freedom, leap upon this so-called proof of harmlessness to support legalization of marijuana.

There is some considerable evidence that marijuana is not so harmless as many presume. Since 1969, when the federal government began making marijuana of controlled quality available to research scientists, evidence suggesting potential hazards has accumulated. The research has provided strong evidence that, if corroborated, would suggest that marijuana in its various forms may be far more hazardous than was originally suspected.

Obviously, one joint of marijuana—or even a few—will not cause considerable harm to the user. What is indicated is that the effects of marijuana are cumulative and related to the amount of marijuana that is used. Prolonged heavy use of marijuana, or less frequent use of the more potent hashish, is associated with at least six different types of potential hazards. The research indicates that cannabis (the generic term for both hashish and marijuana) may:
—cause chromosome damage that could affect the health of the user;
—cause disruption of cellular metabolism, including synthesis of DNA, and may interfere with the functioning of the immune system;
—mimic hormones or act on hormonal regulators to produce a variety of effects ranging from impotence and temporary sterility to the development of female-like breasts in men;
—with heavy use, severely debilitate the bronchial tract and lungs;
—cause sharp personality changes that lead to a marked deterioration in what is normally considered good mental health;
—cause potentially irreversible brain damage.

This last point is most important.

The evidence for some of these potential hazards is derived from the clinical experience of physicians and psychiatrists with relatively few users. Most investigators recognize that this type of evidence has limitations. The subjects have generally used illicitly obtained cannabis whose potency (and identity) is difficult to assess; many of the subjects have also used other drugs; and a reconstruction of the subject's history of cannabis use relies entirely on the subject's potentially faulty memory.

Thus, the evidence is less reliable than evidence obtained in controlled trials where all aspects of the subject's drug use can be monitored. Nonetheless, clinical observations may provide the only evidence available about long-term use of cannabis. If any of the current evidence suggesting multiple hazards from long-term exposure is corroborated, most investigators would consider it ethically indefensible to subject a volunteer to such exposure in clinical trials. It thus seems quite likely that the evidence of hazard associated with prolonged exposure to cannabis will be the subject of continuing controversy.

After you read the article, you tell your editor that you would like to do some checking of your own because this may not be a definitive view. He agrees and suggests you consult references and authorities for a Sunday feature.

Exercises X: Weather

A. Wind

Police report: High winds last night damaged residences and businesses on State Road 166 near Clovia, a suburb. The winds were estimated at 50 miles an hour at their height, and they touched down for about two minutes at 11 p.m. Most of the damage, totaling $15,000, was to outbuildings. Largest single damage, about $5,000, was to the Crossroads Grocery at Three Corners Junction where all the glass was blown out and merchandise shaken from shelves. Two gas pumps shattered and a storage building flattened. No injuries.

B. Cold

The weather bureau said temperatures over the past 24 hours ranged from 25 at 5 a.m. to 40, the high, at 2 p.m. This was the third straight day of unseasonably cold weather. This morning's temperature of 25 was the lowest for this time of year in 15 years. The all-time low for the date was in 1880, 15 degrees. The all-time high was 69 in 1945. The forecast for today is for lows in the 40s, highs in the 50s and an end to the sudden cold snap.

C. Rain

You work for the UPI bureau in Houston and are told to send out a story about a rainstorm that has struck the city. You are told to write about 200 words. The information:

1. Rain began to fall at 1 p.m. Continued for seven hours. Total fall, more than 7½ inches, which some people say is total rainfall for the year in some parts of Texas.
2. Hardest hit area southeast of Houston where Texas Medical Center is located.
3. Creeks and bayous flooded out of banks and streets were flooded and motorists stranded. Still too early to tell if there are any casualties, but no word of any so far.
4. To baseball fans, this was a disaster. For first time in the history of Astrodome, built in 1965, the Houston Astros baseball team had to call off the game. Not because wet grounds; dome covers field. But only a couple of hundred hardy fans reached the park.
5. "We couldn't have gone on anyway," says a dome official. "Half the players weren't here before the game either. The bat boy would have had to bat cleanup if we'd played."

Part 5 Laws and Codes

---

16 Libel, Ethics and Taste

Discussion

A. Libel and Privacy

How would you handle the following material? Give reasons for your decisions:

1. An out-of-state congressman who is campaigning for the Democratic candidate for congress in your district says at a local campaign rally that the Republican candidate is "a failed businessman, unable to make a living, looking for the soft cushion."
2. A witness in a murder trial says the police beat her when they arrived at the scene of a killing. She says in her testimony that one of the two policemen was black. (The record of the incident contains the names of the two patrolmen. You know them. They are white.)
3. A city councilman states at a council meeting that he has been offered a bribe by a local contractor, Jeff Chang, owner of Chang & Sons.
4. A state legislator's monthly newsletter carries an article by the legislator stating that an architect, Bernard McDonnell, hired as a consultant for expansion of the state Supreme Court Building, is a gross incompetent and barely passed his state licensing examination.
5. The district attorney tells you he will file charges tomorrow against a teacher who, a student asserts, sexually molested her.
6. A grand jury reports that four local attorneys are part of an interstate baby-for-sale operation that nets $1 million a year. The four attorneys are named.

7. You have conducted a lengthy interview with a famous rock star who is in town for a concert. You have heard rumors that he had recently been released from an expensive German clinic that specializes in narcotics rehabilitation. He refuses to comment on it, but you know he was out of circulation for three months and a national publication made a veiled reference to his cocaine addiction.

8. The attorney general tells you that a candidate for the state supreme court fathered an illegitimate daughter 30 years ago and supported her for 21 years until her marriage. You cannot quote him, but it is in the candidate's files the local bar association has, he says.

9. A man testifying before a state legislative committee in favor of payments to indigent women seeking abortions has, you learn, served 30 days in jail for "reckless endangerment" in connection with an abortion that he supposedly helped perform 15 years ago.

10. A man, accused of possession of a large amount of heroin, is being defended by a lawyer whose clients include men accused and convicted of drug possession and sales, vice operations and gambling in a tri-state area, and worthless securities sales. He is known among lawyers around the state as "the Mafia's man." Can you identify him this way in a story?

B. Ethics

Discuss the journalistic ethics involved in the following situations:

1. Your editor has told you to get a story on a local men's club that is discussing the admission of women to membership. The meeting is closed, but an adjoining room is vacant and you can hear the discussion from it. Should you listen in?

2. You are a sports reporter covering participant sports, and the manager of a local bowling alley that is on your beat offers to buy you a drink on your rounds; buy you lunch. Do you accept?

3. You are a consumer reporter doing a check on local auto repair shops. Upon completion, you ask a local association of automobile dealers for a comment, and the executive director says that he will advise his members to pull their advertising if you print the story. What do you do?

4. An executive session is being held by the local Independent Party to select a candidate for mayor. You can hear the closed-door discussions across an air shaft; you can hear it better if you toss a small microphone on a long cable over the air shaft to a window sill and record the discussion. Do you listen in?

5. A good source has told you that he can obtain a document about candidates for the job of city manager, including their personal records. Do you ask him to slip you the material?

6. You cover city hall. A local wrestling promoter has asked the sports editor to recommend someone who can write weekly news releases on the wrestling matches in the two-state area the promoter covers, and the editor gives him your name. He offers you the job. Do you take it?

7. A source inside the police department who has given you considerable information not otherwise available was transferred from the vice squad to a low-level desk job for an infraction. He indicates that if you run a story about him you have lost him as a source. Do you write it?

8. You cover the state legislature and develop some personal friends among legislators and lobbyists. They have a friendly weekly poker game and invite you to join them as a regular. Do you?

9. You are going over data on homicides and other violent crimes for the past year, and you notice that race and ethnic origin are included in the homicide figures but not in the rape data. You ask for the data and the police chief says that the department keeps it but has not distributed it because it is "volatile." You obtain the material and understand what he means. Almost 80 percent of the rape arrests involve members of minority groups. As in the case of homicides, the bulk of the victims were of the same race or ethnic origin as the alleged perpetrators. The chief warns you about using the rape data. "Murder is one thing. People can accept it. But rape. . . ." Do you use all the figures?

10. You cover business and finance. A local banker suggests you buy stock in his parent bank because of an expansion program yet unannounced. Do you buy?

11. Your newspaper, you learn from a confidential source, hired a CIA agent in the 1970s and gave him cover as a reporter. What is your obligation?

12. The local chapter of a medical organization is willing to finance your way to the annual convention of the American Medical Association because of the splendid way you have handled medical news over the past year. Your newspaper would like you to go but cannot afford the $1,500 in costs, the editor says. He tells you to use your judgment about accepting the offer. Do you go?

13. A reporter is asked out for an evening—dinner and the theater—by a source. The evening is a social engagement; it is not related to any story the reporter is covering. The reporter is attracted to the source, an attractive, friendly person. Should the reporter accept?

14. A source close to a federal government contract tells you that he has been involved in an illegal scheme to inflate costs. He names two other company officials, who deny the allegations. Your source gives you some documents that allude to the scheme but do not prove it. It is his word against theirs, and you believe him on the basis of long acquaintance. You know that if you run the story he will be fired.

15. You learn that the newspaper plant (or broadcast station property) is vastly under-assessed. You plan to include this in a story about evaluation of downtown property. The editor sends the story upstairs, and mention of the newspaper (or station) is edited out. What do you do?

C. Taste

1. Chapter 16 has a photograph of a graduating student at a urinal. Apply some principles that guide decisions on taste to the picture and draw a conclusion as to whether the picture should have been used.

2. Examine some recent issues of the local and regional newspapers and some news magazines. Do you see any stories or pictures that raise questions about the use of language or subject matter? If so, cut out the material, apply some of the textbook's guidelines on the use of such material and take to class.

3. There is increasing criticism of the media for a general "loosening of standards." Often, this refers to the liberal use of obscenity and profanity and the explicit description of crime and sexual matters. Interview the following people and see whether you can develop a consensus of community views:

   a. Religious leader (priest, minister, rabbi).

   b. News director of local station, managing editor of local newspaper. Reporter.

   c. Teacher of U.S. history, sociology, psychology.

   d. Parents of grade school students.

   e. High school newspaper editor.

   f. Head of local Chamber of Commerce, Bar Association, Medical Society, construction workers union.

Index

wcb
Wm. C. Brown Company Publishers
Dubuque, Iowa

ISBN 0-697-043

Workbook:
Basic News Writing

Melvin Mencher